A Birding Miscellany

An eclectic collection of lists and facts all about birds.

By Ian Parsons

With illustrations by Jo Parsons

"A bird does not sing because it has an answer. It sings because it has a song." *Chinese Proverb*

Contents

Acknowledgements

There are many people that have directly or indirectly helped me in the writing of this book. I won't attempt to thank them all individually but suffice to say I am grateful to you all. Many have been unwitting in giving their help, forced to listen to me reeling off yet another interesting snippet of information, but their positive response to this is what inspired me to put this book together in the first place. So, if you have ever had me go off on a tangent about birds then I thank you for patiently listening.

Special thanks must go to Guy Rippon and Verna Kocaj, I don't know how many hundreds of conversations we have had between us about birds (often over a beer or three) but your enthusiasm and support for me and my birding ideas has been endless. In particular I owe Verna a huge debt of gratitude for her patient and methodical correction of my spelling, grammar and punctuation on the draft of this book – must try harder next time! Needless to say that if there are any errors found they are entirely my fault.

Finally, thank you to Jo for always being there. I couldn't do this without you.

Introduction

Ever since I was a small child I have been fascinated by birds and wildlife. Growing up in the county of Devon, the ample access to the countryside and coast gave me many opportunities to find out more about the natural world. As I approached my teens I also became fascinated by trivia, if there was an interesting fact about something I liked then I wanted to know it!

My interest in birds really developed at college and I was able to apply this interest during my 20 years working in conservation and subsequently in my bird tour business, Griffon Holidays, which is based in the birding heaven of Extremadura in central Spain. Combining my love of trivia with my love of birds happened without me realising it, but as my tour clients and people who have been on the many guided walks I have led over the years will attest, it is a combination that I am always ready to share!

This book is the fruit of my love for birds and trivia. It is aimed at anyone who has an interest in birds, be they professional ornithologists or someone who just enjoys watching the Sparrows from their office window. Hopefully you will find it a fun read but also a read that will make you think a bit more about the birds that we see around us.

Birds are fascinating. They are also completely accessible to everyone. Whether you live in the remotest rural hamlet or in the heart of a large City there will be birds living with you. Birds are full of interest no matter how common or how rare they are. Enjoy them and enjoy my collection of trivia, facts and lists all about them.

Ian

See www.griffonholidays.com for more details on birding tours to Extremadura led by Ian. Great birds and no doubt more fascinating facts...

First things first...

Right, let's clear one thing up from the start. Ostriches do not bury their heads in the sand. It was the Roman historian, Pliny the Elder, that started the myth about them doing so and he was completely wrong! However, for some reason, the idea caught on and many people still think it is true. Another little gem from Pliny the Elder was that Ostriches hatched their eggs by looking at them aggressively. This idea didn't catch on...

Pliny the Elder has long gone but the birds are still with us and so is the fascination for understanding their behaviour. Lets start off with looking at their taxonomic status. Or to put it simply, who is related to who...

How Birds fit together from a taxonomic viewpoint

Birds belong to the scientific class of Aves. There used to be several subclasses within Aves but all apart from one have become extinct. All living birds now belong to this subclass, the Neornithines – literally 'modern birds'.

This subclass is then split into two separate superorders:

Subclass	Superorder	Meaning
	Paleognathae	'Ancient Jaws'
Neornithines		
	Neognathae	'New Palate'

Now we humans love order. But, as we look more closely, using modern techniques, we find that sorting birds into a neat system of orders and families isn't as straightforward as we thought. In fact it is very complicated and at times controversial as different experts often disagree where certain birds belong in the taxonomic order. What follows is a generally accepted taxonomic order of modern birds. Definitely subject to change though...

Superorder	Order	Example Family	Example Species
	Struthioniformes	Ostriches	Ostrich (*Struthio camelus*)
	Rheiformes	Rheas	Darwin's Rhea (*Rhea pennata*)
Paleognathae	Tinamiformes	Tinamous	Grey Tinamou (*Tinamus tao*)
	Casuariiformes	Cassowaries	Southern Cassowary (*Casuarius casuarius*)
	Apterygiformes	Kiwis	Roroa (*Apteryx haastii*)

Superorder	Order	Example Family	Example Species
	Anseriformes	Ducks	Mallard (*Anas platyrhynchos*)
	Galliformes	Grouse	Rock Ptarmigan (*Lagopus muta*)
	Podicipediformes	Grebes	Little Grebe (*Tachybaptus ruficollis*)
	Phoenicopteriformes	Flamingos	Lesser Flamingo (*Phoenicopterus minor*)
	Mesitornithiformes	Mesites	Brown Mesite (*Mesitornis unicolor*)
	Pteroclidiformes	Sandgrouse	Painted Sandgrouse (*Pterocles indicus*)
	Columbiformes	Pigeons	Rock Dove (*Columba livia*)
Neognathae	Phaethontiformes	Tropicbirds	Red-billed Tropicbird (*Phaethon aethereus*)
	Caprimulgiformes	Nightjars	European Nightjar (*Caprimulgus europaeus*)
	Apodiformes	Swifts	Alpine Swift (*Apus melba*)
	Aegotheliformes	Owlet-Nightjars	Starry Owlet-Nightjar (*Aegotheles tatei*)
	Cuculiformes	Cuckoos	Common Cuckoo (*Cuculus canorus*)
	Opisthocomiformes	Hoatzin	Hoatzin (*Opisthocomus hoazin*)
	Gruiformes	Bustards	Great Bustard (*Otis tarda*)
	Gaviiformes	Loons	Red-throated Loon (*Gavia stellata*)

Continued over

Superorder	Order	Example Family	Example Species
	Sphenisciformes	Penguins	King Penguin (*Aptenodytes patagonicus*)
	Procellariiformes	Albatrosses	Shy Albatross (*Diomedea cauta*)
	Ciconiiformes	Storks	White Stork (*Ciconia ciconia*)
	Pelecaniformes	Boobies	Masked Booby (*Sula dactylatra*)
	Charadriiformes	Gulls	Common Gull (*Larus canus*)
	Accipitriformes	Eagles	Golden Eagle (*Aquila chrysaetos*)
Neognathae (Cont.)	Strigiformes	Owls	Barn Owl (*Tyto alba*)
	Coliiformes	Mousebirds	Speckled Mousebird (*Colius striatus*)
	Trogoniformes	Trogons	Collared Trogon (*Trogon collaris*)
	Coraciiformes	Hoopoe	Hoopoe (*Upupa epops*)
	Leptosomatiformes	Cuckoo Rollers	Cuckoo Roller (*Leptosomus discolor*)
	Piciformes	Toucans	Toco Toucan (*Ramphastos toco*)
	Falconiformes	Falcons	Peregrine Falcon (*Falco peregrinus*)
	Cariamiformes	Seriemas	Red-legged Seriema (*Cariama cristata*)
	Psittaciformes	Macaws	Scarlet Macaw (*Ara macao*)
	Passeriformes	Thrushes	Redwing (*Turdus iliacus*)

The Language of Birds

In the English language we call them 'birds', but in other languages they are the following:

Language	'Bird'	Language	'Bird'
English	Bird	German	Vogel
Spanish	Ave	Hungarian	Madár
Dutch	Vogel	Icelandic	Fugl
Finnish	Lintu	Italian	Uccello
French	Oiseau	Polish	Ptak
Swedish	Fågel	Welsh	Adar

So a Pied Flycatcher flying into Europe across the Straits of Gibraltar becomes an Ave before becoming an Oiseau, before becoming a Bird before settling into its Welsh Oak valley as an Adar.

Many bird species have been taught to mimic human speech but there is also plenty of evidence to suggest that some have been able to learn actual meanings to words and use them accordingly. The world record for vocabulary goes to a Budgerigar named Puck that had a vocabulary of 1,728 human words...

"...and another thing..."

We humans have also given names to the languages that the birds themselves use. These are the names of bird calls/songs from a few species:

Bird Species	Name of Call/Song	Bird Species	Name of Call/Song
Bittern	Boom	Lapwing	Peewit
Blackbird	Whistle	Linnet	Chuckle
Blackcap	Chick-chack	Magpie	Chatter
Chaffinch	Chirp or Pink	Nightingale	Pipe or Warble or Jug-jug
Crow	Caw	Owl	Hoot or Screech
Cuckoo	Cuckoo	Parrot	Talk
Dove	Coo	Pigeon	Coo
Duck	Quack	Raven	Croak
Eagle	Scream	Rook	Caw
Falcon	Chant	Sparrow	Chirp
Goose	Cackle	Swallow	Twitter
Guineafowl	Come back	Thrush	Whistle
Grouse	Drum	Turkey	Gobble
Hawk	Scream	Vulture	Scream
Jay	Chatter	Whitethroat	Chirr

"I don't know what all the fuss is about, we've been doing it for years"

Breeding and nests

Black-tailed Godwits are migratory waders that pair for life. However, the pairs break up for the winter when the different sexes migrate to different wintering sites often over a hundred miles apart. Somehow, when they return to their breeding grounds they manage to synchronise their arrivals to within 3 days of each other despite the fact that the arrival period for the species at its breeding grounds spans a month. It is not known how they seem to know when each other will arrive but one thing is for certain, they can't be too late as the bird that arrives first will find another partner if the other fails to arrive within a few days.

Several birds, including Nightjars and Plovers, will fake injury in an attempt to lure predators away from their nest sites. The idea being that the predator will have its interest captured by the prospect of an easy meal (the 'injured' bird) and will then follow it. Once the 'injured' bird feels confident that it has guided the predator away from its nest it stages a miracle recovery and flies off leaving behind a confused and hungry predator.

Barnacle Geese don't rush into a relationship. First and second year birds spend time socialising with similar aged birds of the opposite sex. They select a favourite and will then spend several days with their prospective partner before either moving on to another or choosing them. Most birds spend time getting to know at least two others before they find 'The One'. They then settle into a monogamous relationship with their new partner.

Woodpigeons have been shown to positively select nest sites near to the nest sites of the Hobby. The Hobby is a small Falcon that is well known for vigorously defending its nest territory from other, bigger, birds of prey. On seeing an intruding raptor the Hobby takes to the air calling noisily and diving at the bird until it drives it off. Species regularly chased off by the Hobby include the Goshawk, Peregrine Falcon and Sparrowhawk all three of which will happily predate Woodpigeons. It seems as though the Woodpigeon selects nest sites close to the Hobby to benefit directly from this behaviour. Although the Hobby is a predator the pigeon has nothing to fear from its neighbour as the Hobby feeds mainly on flying insects and small birds.

The actual act of mating for a bird can be a dangerous thing. Whilst engaged in the act they are extremely vulnerable to potential predators. Mating therefore tends to be a very brief act, often over in less than a second for many species. The Vasa Parrot of Madagascar however takes its time and have been known to mate for an hour and a half!

In species where mating is very brief it can often also be very frequent. A female of the Smith's Longspur of North America was recorded having 629 matings in just over 6 days...

Some species need to be in a colony to breed. It is known for instance that captive Flamingos have greater breeding success in zoos when they are tricked into thinking that they are part of a larger colony by the use of mirrors. It is believed that the now sadly extinct Passenger Pigeon, which in just a few decades went from being one of the most abundant birds in the world to complete extinction, was a species that needed the stimulus of being in a large breeding colony to successfully produce young. As their vast numbers reduced due to mankind hunting them and destroying their habitat so their colonies reduced to below a critical size for breeding. Even though the remaining colonies may have been of several hundred birds it would appear that they just weren't big enough to stimulate breeding activity. What might be called an Exhibitionist Extinction.

Many species of birds are often thought as being truly monogamous but modern DNA studies have shown that this isn't necessarily the case. Even those that are monogamous in their mating behaviour have their ups and downs. It is thought that each year about 10% of Oystercatcher pairs 'divorce' and find new mates. Normally it is the female that initiates proceedings by quite simply flying off. It is thought that, among other reasons, the males ability to procure plenty of food for his mate is key to the relationship lasting.

The female Greater Roadrunner is by no means a cheap date. If her male partner wants to mate with her he has to come bearing gifts in the form of food (often a small lizard or scorpion). No food no mating is the general rule.

The Willow Ptarmigan and its British race the Red Grouse are more successful at breeding if they mate with a bird of similar social standing. Birds that mate with an 'equal' fledge more young than birds that mate with birds of a higher or lower social rank than themselves.

"...It will never work..."

Other female birds will use mating as a means to an end with some species offering a mating in exchange for nest material etc. One species, the Purple-throated Hummingbird, will offer to mate with males, even out of the breeding season, in exchange for access to his territory and the nectar producing flowers within it. Unsurprisingly, the male seems happy to allow this to happen.

Penduline Tits have a different breeding strategy to most. The male makes wonderful nests to attract his mate but as soon as he thinks the female has laid her clutch he up sticks and goes off to make more nests to attract new mates, leaving his first mate to rear the brood herself. However, the female also tries to leave the male to look after the brood by concealing that she has started laying by hiding the eggs in the nest lining. If she can complete her clutch without the male realising it she will leave to find a new mate, leaving the male with a nest full of eggs which he then rears by himself.

Ground nesting birds often conceal themselves from predators with the aid of camouflage, their cryptic colours helping them remain hidden from prying eyes. However, several predators hunt by scent as well as by sight and many ground nesting birds have therefore evolved cryptic scent. Normally, when preening, birds secrete a wax like substance to keep their feathers in tip top condition, however the chemical compounds in the wax are relatively smelly and would readily attract the attention of a keen nosed predator. When breeding, many ground nesting birds are able to change the chemical make up of their wax to one that is much less smelly and therefore less noticeable to predators.

It has been shown that many birds will select nest sites close to the nests of aggressive insects like wasps. It is believed that this is done so that the wasps act as a deterrent to would be nest predators and parasites. It's probably quite a good deterrent for would be bird ringers as well!!

Long-tailed Tits make wonderful dome shaped nests out of moss and lichens that they bind together using spider webs. In all, the nest is often made up of 6,000 pieces of material, it is then lined with feathers, lots and lots of them. Many nests contain over 2,000 feathers! Someone actually counted them.

On a counting theme the Black Woodpecker (Europe's largest Woodpecker) makes its nest by chiselling out an entrance hole and chamber within a tree trunk leaving the woodland floor beneath it covered in woodchips. Someone, and it may or may not have been the same person who counted the feathers above, counted these chips and found that there were over 10,000 of them under one nest. Not sure who had the biggest headache, the woodpecker or the person who did the counting!

Not all birds build an actual nest, European Nightjars for example lay their eggs on a bare patch of ground. The Emperor Penguin lays its egg on to their feet where they proceed to incubate it.

Other birds though go to the opposite extreme and build superbly intricate nests of architectural brilliance and, hey, if it looks good why just build the one? That certainly seems to be the idea of many species of Weaver bird where the males will make several amazing nest structures in an attempt to lure a female into mating with him and using one of the nests.

It is well known that young chicks in a nest instantly open their brightly coloured gapes to solicit food from the adults when they arrive at the nest. The open gape has long been known to be a stimulus for the adult triggering it to feed the young. A recent study showed that perhaps there is a bit more to it than that though. Chicks that have brighter red gapes than their siblings get more food and, in one species, a study showed that the redness of the gape could be linked to the strength of the birds immune system and therefore by feeding the chicks with the brighter gapes the adult birds were investing the most energy in the healthiest chicks. However, another study, this time in Linnets, has shown that the red gapes of the chicks lessen in brightness when they have just been fed, this would appear to show the adults which chicks have just been fed and which chicks require to be fed.

The European Coot is well known for being a little bit grumpy, often driving off other species of bird for no apparent reason. Unfortunately for its young it can also be a rather grumpy parent too. If it feels that a chick is misbehaving, perhaps begging for food incessantly for example, it will grab them hard in its bill, shake them vigorously and even hold them underwater. This is often enough rough treatment to kill the chick. Those that survive often go off on their own to hide which in turn can prove fatal as without their parents they are extremely vulnerable to predation. Coots lay large clutches of eggs but only a few chicks survive to fledging probably due to this 'parenting' behaviour.

About a fifth of all bird species have chicks that weigh more than the adults at fledging time. This isn't a result of over feeding by the parents it's a deliberate strategy to help the chicks survive the difficult post fledging period.

The Hamerkop of Africa makes several nests in a season, even when not breeding, whilst not as intricately built as those of the Weaver Bird the nests are absolutely huge. They can measure up to 1.5 metres across and be composed of over 10,000 individual sticks (that same person again?), the structure has a domed roof and a mud lined tunnel leading to the nest chamber. The nests are often strong enough to take a persons weight. All of this for a bird that measures less than 60cms in length and weighs less than half a kilo!

Male Australian Bower birds go to great lengths to impress females, building structures of elaborate design and decor. Different species go for different designs; some go for avenues, some for teepees others for chambers. They decorate them with a whole host of bright shiny objects that they pick up from their surroundings. Nowadays many of these surroundings contain humans and often many of the objects that the birds decorate their bowers with are of human origin including one report of a glass eye being used (how?!). But these structures shouldn't be confused with nests. They are shameless bachelor pads and the male birds are shameless players. Once they have enticed a female into their bower, they quickly mate with her and then encourage her to leave so that he can tidy up and then entice another female in. Once mated the females go off and build a nest for their clutch which they then raise all by themselves – the males are far too busy living their bachelor lifestyle to be interested in such mundane matters.

Eleonora's Falcon is a highly specialised breeder. Nesting on islands in the Mediterranean it times its breeding to coincide with the post breeding migration of European passerines. The Falcon doesn't start to lay its eggs until late July, by the time these hatch it is late August and the autumn passage of passerines is well under way. The adult falcons fly out over the sea together to intercept the migrating birds, many of which are exhausted. Over the sea the small birds have no escape and the falcons will coordinate with one another to tire out a selected bird until it is easily caught by one of the falcons. It is then taken back to the hungry chicks in the nest. The Falcons are not fussy about which species they feed on with nearly 100 species of bird being recorded as prey items. The Eleonora's Falcon is highly specialised in breeding and hunting strategies but it is definitely a generalist when it comes to prey selection.

The Tailor birds are a group of small birds that get their name from their nests. After selecting a branch with large leaves on it, they poke holes in the leaf edges with their bills and then, using spider webs or plant fibres, they stitch the large leaves together sewing them in to a cone shape structure in which they then construct their nests. Because the leaves are still attached to the tree and the holes for the stitches are so tiny, the leaves carry on living without discolouring at all providing excellent camouflage for the nest hidden within them.

Eggsceptional Facts...

The non head burying Ostrich maybe one of the largest birds in existence but it lays the smallest egg of any bird pro rata to its body weight. Ostrich eggs are only 1.5% of an adult females bodyweight. The Winter Wren, one of Europe's smallest birds, lays eggs that weigh 13% of an adult females bodyweight. The unfortunate bird that lays the heaviest egg pro rata to its body weight is the Little Spotted Kiwi of New Zealand. Its egg weighs 26% of an adult females bodyweight! Now if an Ostrich laid an egg that was 26% of its body weight it could weigh up to 30kgs!

The largest single cell in the natural world is the yolk of an Ostrich egg. These big cells require a big egg to protect them. Mankind has long exploited these large eggshells and used them (as many nomadic tribes do today) as water carriers. Not only is the egg a useful way to carry water but it would appear that it is also a healthy one too as the shells have anti-bacterial properties that keep the water free of nasties.

Showing their Reptilian history, the Australian Brush Turkey can determine what sex its young will be by regulating the incubation temperature of their eggs. Once a female lays her eggs they are buried under large mounds of earth by both adults. These mounds generate heat and the adult bird can regulate this by removing or adding soil as necessary. At lower temperatures more males hatch whilst at higher temperatures more females hatch. It is not known whether this is done as a deliberate way to adjust the sex ratio or not.

The Pied Flycatcher of Europe lays pale blue eggs, the brighter the colour of the egg the more likely the chick that hatches from it will survive. Studies have shown that chicks from brighter eggs have healthier immune systems.

The extinct Elephant Bird laid the biggest eggs ever known to man, they were over 30cms in length and probably weighed around 10kgs, roughly the same as 10,000 hummingbird eggs.

The eggs of the Guillemot, a sea bird from Europe, are specially shaped to avoid falling off the bare cliff ledge that the adults breed on. The shape of them is such that if they roll at all they just roll in very small circles rather than rolling any distance – a potential issue when nesting on narrow cliff ledges!

The family of birds known as the Megapodes (of which the Australian Brush Turkey is a member) and the Kiwis are the only birds whose chicks have to hatch out of their eggs without the aid of an egg tooth. An egg tooth is a small, hard and sharp protuberance on the still developing bill of the young bird, using a special muscle in its neck the chick is able to push this egg tooth against the inside of the egg with enough force to break it. The Kiwis though use their legs and the Megapodes use their claws.

Canadian scientists have discovered that when pop music is played to chickens they increase their egg production. No one knows why and so far no one has tried to see if this works on wild birds.

Bird brain!

We humans often use the term bird brain as an insult yet we use the image of an Owl as a symbol of wisdom??? Is that clever?

The eyes of the Ostrich weigh more than its brain, in fact the brain of the Ostrich is the smallest brain of any bird when measured pro rata with its body size. Parrots have the largest brain pro rata to their weight. But, the corvids (Crow family) have the largest cerebral hemispheres per body size of any bird and this would imply that they have a greater capacity to think and solve. Examples of the corvids apparently thinking and solving include:

- The New Caledonian Crow, which, on finding a nice juicy beetle grub in a hole in a tree branch will fly off and find a twig of the right length and diameter so that it can winkle its lunch out of the hole. However, if it is unable to find the perfect twig it will select one and manufacture it until it is the right size for the job. Manufacturing tools has been seen in the higher apes (including ourselves of course) but wasn't thought to occur elsewhere in the animal kingdom.

- The Raven has long been reputed to be an intelligent bird. Studies have shown that if a Raven finds a food source that it can't consume in one sitting and is then spotted by a second Raven, the first will intentionally lead the second away before giving it the slip and returning to finish its meal.

- Clark's Nutcracker caches huge numbers of pine seeds in the ground to use as a food resource at a later date. It has been estimated that one bird can cache as many as 98,000 seeds in a year. It would appear to deliberately over cache, possibly as an insurance against other animals finding some of them. The bird demonstrates great memory recall as it has been shown to find these caches many months later even when the area is buried under a layer of snow.

- The Eastern race of Carrion Crow that occurs in Japan has discovered that Walnuts make good eating. The problem for the bird is that its bill is not strong enough to open them. Some Crows have solved this problem by waiting at traffic lights and when the light is red and the traffic stationary they nip down and place them amongst the traffic. When the lights go green the traffic moves and smashes the nutshells. It would appear that the Crows have also learnt the significance of the traffic light colours as they wait until the lights return to red before flying down and safely gathering their reward.

The Greater Honeyguide of Africa is a bird with an unusual diet, it likes to eat Beeswax. The problem for the bird is that the beeswax is contained in bee nests and these are too difficult for the bird to break into. The bird readily feeds at nests which have been broken into by man and animals such as the Ratel, however the behaviour it is best known for is the guiding of humans to wild bee nests. It would appear the species has learnt that humans on encountering a wild bees nest, will break it open therefore allowing the bird to reach its favourite food. To guide someone it attracts their attention by calling repeatedly in front of them, in this manner it then guides them in the direction of a nest. Once the person has broken and collected the honey the wax is easily accessible to the bird. Many native tribes in Africa have the tradition of thanking the bird with honey, they believe that if they didn't the next time the bird guides them it might lead them straight to a lion or a snake.

A study by two Canadian scientists based in France would appear to show that birds are capable of understanding speed limits. On roads with higher speed limits birds that were feeding on the road edge would fly away earlier than when feeding on roads with lower speed limits implying that they recognise that traffic travels at different speeds on different roads.

A Flock of Birds or should that be A Dissimulation of Birds or perhaps A Volery of Birds...

The following is a list of nouns used to describe groups of birds, some are rather dull, some rather obvious whilst others are just a bit bizarre or in the case of Guillemot, bazaar!

BIRD	GROUP NAME
Bittern	Sedge *or* Siege
Bobolink	Chain
Budgerigar	Chatter
Buzzard	Wake
Capercailie	Tok
Chicken	Brood
Chough	Chattering
Coot	Covert
Cormorant	Flight
Crane	Sedge *or* Siege *or* Herd
Crow	Murder *or* Storytelling
Curlew	Herd
Dotterel	Trip
Dove	Piteousness *or* Flight *or* Dole *or* Cote *or* Bevy *or* Dule
Duck (in flight)	Flush *or* Pump *or* Team
Duck (on ground)	Badelynge
Duck (on water)	Paddling *or* Raft
Dunlin	Flight
Eagle	Convocation *or* Aerie
Emu	Mob
Falcon	Cast
Finches	Charm
Flamingo	Flurry *or* Regiment
Geese (in flight)	Skein *or* Wedge
Geese (on ground)	Gaggle

BIRD	GROUP NAME
Goldfinch	Charm *or* Vein
Grouse (pair)	Brace
Guillemots	Bazaar
Gull	Colony
Hawk	Cast *or* Kettle *or* Aerie
Heron	Sedge *or* Siege *or* Hedge
Hoopoe	Happiness
Hummingbird	Charm *or* Hover
Ibis	Crowd
Jay	Scolding *or* Band *or* Party
Lapwing	Deceit
Lark	Exaltation *or* Ascension
Magpie	Tiding *or* Tittering
Mallard	Flush *or* Sword
Nightingale	Watch
Owl	Parliament *or* Wisdom
Oxbird	Fling
Parrot	Company
Partridge	Covey
Passenger Pigeon (now extinct)	Roost
Peacock	Muster *or* Ostentation
Penguin	Rookery *or* Colony *or* Creche *or* Parcel *or* Huddle
Pheasants	Nye *or* Bouquet
Pigeon	Flight *or* Flock
Plovers	Congregation
Pochard	Rush
Ptarmigan	Covey
Quail	Bevy *or* Covey
Raven	Unkindness *or* Conspiracy *or* Storytelling
Rook	Clamour *or* Building *or* Parliament *or* Storytelling

BIRD	GROUP NAME
Ruff	Hill
Sandpiper	Fling
Shelduck	Dopping
Snipe	Wisp *or* Walk
Sparrow	Host
Starling	Murmuration *or* Chatter *or* Scourge
Stork	Muster *or* Mustering
Swallow	Flight
Swan (in flight)	Wedge
Swan	Herd *or* Bevy *or* Ballet *or* Lamentation
Swift	Flock
Teal	Spring
Thrush	Mutation
Turkey	Rafter *or* Flock
Turtle Dove	Pitying
Wigeon	Company *or* Knob

"How can we be both a wisdom and a parliament?!?!"

Domestic Bliss?

There are estimated to be 10,000 species of bird on the planet, so far mankind has only truly domesticated just 0.1% of them, or in other words 10 of them to create 9 truly domesticated birds. Here they are with their original wild versions.

Domesticated Form	Original Species
Chicken	Red Junglefowl (*Gallus gallus*)
Duck	Mallard (*Anas platyrhnchos*)
Pigeon	Rock Dove (*Columba livia*)
Guinea Fowl	Helmeted Guineafowl (*Numida melegris*)
Ringneck Dove	African Collared Dove (*Streptopelia roseogrisea*)
Turkey	Wild Turkey (*Meleagris gallopavo*)
Canary	Atlantic Canary (*Serinus canaria*)
Society Finch	White-rumped Munia (*Lonchura striata*)
Goose	Greylag Goose (*Anser anser*) and Swan Goose (*Anser cygnoides*)

The Dog and Duck

Many English pubs are named after birds including the legendary Dog and Duck. Here are twenty examples, why not try and tick them - but perhaps not all in one go... Drink in moderation – only have a *swift* half.

PUB NAME	☑
The Barn Owl	
The White Swan	
The Black Swan	
The Swan with 2 Necks	
The Duck Inn	
The Pelican	
The Three Cranes	
The Three Pigeons	
The Rat and Parrot	
The Goose and Granite	
The Nightingale	
The Kingfisher	
The Crow's Nest	
The Eagle and Child	
The Woodcock	
The Seagull	
The Peacock	
The Ostrich	
The Woodpecker	
The Raven	

Game Birds?

The names of birds are often used by sports teams as nicknames, sometimes the species chosen has similar plumage to the team and at other times the name would appear to have been chosen to imply that the team has similar characteristics... Watching football nowadays you have to wonder why none are named after the Divers.
Here are a few:

ENGLISH FOOTBALL

TEAM NAME	NICKNAME
Bradford City	The Bantams
Brighton and Hove Albion	The Seagulls
Bristol City	The Robins
Cardiff City	The Bluebirds
Crystal Palace	The Eagles
Newcastle United	The Magpies
Norwich City	The Canaries
Sheffield Wednesday	The Owls
Swansea City	The Swans
Torquay United	The Gulls

NORTH AMERICAN FOOTBALL

TEAM NAME	NICKNAME
Baltimore	Ravens
Philadelphia	Eagles
Atlanta	Falcons
Arizona	Cardinals
Seattle	Seahawks

NORTH AMERICAN BASEBALL

TEAM NAME	NICKNAME
Baltimore	Orioles
St. Louis	Cardinals
Toronto	Blue Jays

ENGLISH CRICKET T20

TEAM NAME	NICKNAME
Derbyshire	Falcons
Essex	Eagles

"Not sure this is the best name really...."

Food for thought...

The Lesser Rhea has the latin name of *Rhea darwinii* after Charles Darwin sent part of the bird's carcass back to the Zoological Society of London from his famous HMS Beagle expedition. Darwin sent the head, neck, legs, a wing, some feathers and most of the skin. Unusually most of it was cooked – it was the remains of his dinner! The story goes that Darwin, whilst settling down to his meal of what was thought to be a juvenile Greater Rhea, realised that the anatomy of the bird was so different that it must in fact be a different species.

Birds that associate with humans often end up eating all sorts of bizarre items. An Ostrich in London Zoo was found to have eaten a 1m length of rope, 3 gloves, a comb, a camera film, a pencil, a handkerchief, several coins, most of a gold necklace, a watch and an alarm clock. Who takes an alarm clock to a zoo?

It has been estimated that an average baby European Robin eats 4 metres of earthworms everyday!

The Burrowing Owl of America is a generalist feeder but some particularly enjoy Dung Beetles. To make their life easier they will fly around their territory and collect various bits of dung which they then arrange close to a suitable perch where they then wait for the Dung Beetles to come to them.

Birds nest soup is made from the nests of Asian Swiftlets. The nests are made entirely from the saliva of the bird as well as a few particles of dust that get entwined in the structure. Dirty spit is apparently a delicacy.

When life is easy some birds, a bit like some humans, will get fat but, as soon as life gets harder again they will lose it rapidly. Great Tits living in areas without Sparrowhawks weigh more than those that live in areas where Sparrowhawks are present. The heavier birds can get away with being a little bit less agile than their hunted relations.

The bill of the Lesser Flamingo is a highly specialist filter. On average the bird uses it to filter 20 litres of water a day, the filter effect catches tiny particles of food such as algae. It is estimated that each litre of water filtered produces 3grams of food.

It was always thought that us mammals were the only animals that fed their young on their own body secretions (i.e. milk). But it is now known that many birds also do this. Storm Petrels, Shearwaters, Albatrosses, Flamingos, Pigeons, and even some Penguins, all secrete a liquid from the wall of their gut which they then feed to their young either mixed in with other food or on its own.

The Hawfinch of Europe may be a small bird weighing on average a mere 55 grams but, using its large bill, it can exert a force of 50 kilograms (almost 1,000 times heavier than the bird) to crack open Cherry and Olive stones to get at the nutritious food that lies within them. Don't try that at home unless you have good dental insurance...

The colourful European Bee-eater eats Bees (surprising really). But Bees have stings and stings hurt so the bird removes the sting before swallowing it or feeding it to its young by flying off to a favourite perch where it then smears the rear end of the Bee along it removing the sting in the process.

Pelicans have enormous pouches of skin as part of their bills that enable them to scoop large quantities of food up on their dives. The larger species can hold up to 11kg of fish in their pouch, about the same as their body weight!

The Hooded Pitohui, a bird from Papua New Guinea, eats so many poisonous beetles that its feathers and skin become deadly poisonous, containing the same sort of poison that the infamous poison arrow frogs produce. It is believed that this might be a deliberate defence mechanism against predators including humans. The native name for the bird is the Rubbish Bird, a reference to the fact that they can't eat it.

Green Herons of America often go fishing for their prey. They bait the water surface with insects which attracts the fish to within their reach and then they strike.

Grebes eat small fish that have sharp bones and spines. To protect their stomachs they line them with feathers which form a felt like layer in their stomach. The first food a baby Grebe receives from its parent is feathers from the parents breast for this purpose.

"Just lining my stomach"

It is well known that Hummingbirds live life on the very limits of existence, they can't afford to waste time and energy if they are to survive. The Rufous Hummingbird of America not only knows where to find the nectar rich flowers that lie within its territory but it also appears to know when it last fed from them. Rather than wasting time and energy feeding from half full flowers it only feeds on flowers that have had time to completely restock their nectar store.

Many birds swallow food to take back to their young where they then regurgitate it for the chicks to feed on. The King Penguin of Antarctica does this too but unlike other birds it can take the penguin up to 3 weeks to get back to the chick. The King Penguin has the unique ability of storing food, undigested, in its stomach where it is also prevented from going off so that the chick gets 'fresh' food when it is finally delivered.

After catching a fish the Osprey will manoeuvre it in its talons so that it faces head first into the airflow. Because fish are streamlined to head through water headfirst this minimises the drag making flying with the fish easier for the bird.

The Puffin of the North Atlantic feeds its youngsters on Sand Eels which it catches individually. To minimise travelling time the Puffin doesn't go straight back to its nest burrow as soon as it catches one. They have the ability to hold previous caught eels in their bill whilst they catch a new one, in this way they can build up quite a catch before undertaking the journey back to their young. One Puffin was recorded with 60 eels in its bill!

Other than being birds, the Song Thrush of Europe and the Lammergeier Vulture don't at first glance appear to share too many traits. However they both have adopted a similar feeding method. The Song Thrush loves to eat snails but snails come in a hard protective shell, the thrushes get around this by smashing the snails against a stone to get at the juicy insides. The Lammergeier loves to eat bone marrow but bone marrow comes in a hard protective bone, the vultures get around this by smashing the bones on to rocks to get at the juicy insides. Often both the Song Thrush and the Lammergeier will have their favourite stone/rocks for this purpose and both will fly considerable distances from where they find their food to get to their favourite smashing site.

Many Vultures have featherless heads and necks so that they can stick their bills right into large corpses to get at the choicest bits without clogging their feathers with sticky gunk!

The Hoatzin of South America eat leaves. Leaves are not easily digested and to help the process the bird has a specially adapted foregut that uses bacteria to ferment the leaves before they pass to the stomach. This is a very similar process to that used by the ruminant mammals such as sheep. Hoatzins are the only bird species that has this digestive process.

The American Bushtit, a tiny relative of the European Long-tailed Tit, is so tiny that it needs to constantly feed to survive. It needs to find and eat 80% of its body weight everyday just to avoid hyperthermia. That would be the equivalent of the 'average' person eating 60 kilograms of food every day!

It is well known that members of the Shrike family will impale their food (mainly insects but also including frogs, lizards, small mammals, birds etc) on to the thorns of trees or on to the barbs of barbed wire, storing them like a larder for later consumption. It has long been known to us humans that as the food dries out it also improves nutritionally as well but this was thought to be an incidental effect of the Shrikes behaviour and not the cause of it. Recent studies though have shown that the Shrike could be deliberately drying the food to improve the nutritional value of it. When trying to solicit mating from a female a male shrike will offer the female a gift of dried food rather than a freshly caught item, this would seem to imply that the male is aware of the greater 'value' of the item.

There is an American Woodpecker that is very well named. The Acorn Woodpecker eats Acorns. But acorns are seasonal in their appearance, so, like many birds, they cache them when they are in abundance to feed on them when times are harder. Their acorn caches are a communal affair, they pick a tree, chisel out a hole in the trunk with their bill and then stash the acorn in it. They match the acorn to the exact sized hole so that it is firmly in place, as the acorn dries out and shrinks they move it to a smaller hole so that there is no risk of it dropping out. Some of these caches are huge with up to 50,000 acorns all stored in individual holes all over the trunk.

Biggest, Fastest, Tallest, etc

The biggest and tallest living bird is the Ostrich, it can be up to 2.8 metres tall and weigh up to 115kgs. But the tallest bird ever is the extinct Moa of New Zealand which reached up to 3.5 metres tall. The heaviest bird ever is the extinct Elephant Bird of Madagascar that weighed up to 450kgs

The tallest living flying bird is the Sarus Crane with birds living in India reaching 1.8 metres in height, whilst the heaviest living flying bird is the Great Bustard with a male from north east China weighing in at 21kgs. The heaviest seabirds are the Great White Pelican and the Dalmatian Pelican that can both weigh up to 15kgs.

At the other end of the size spectrum is the smallest living bird, the Bee Hummingbird of Cuba that weighs less than 2gms and measures between 5 and 6cms in length.

Therefore the largest living bird weighs 57,500 times as heavy as the smallest living bird.

The fastest bird is the Peregrine Falcon which has been recorded reaching speeds of 242mph/389kph during a stoop. The Golden Eagle comes in second with speeds of 200mph/320kph recorded during a stoop. But both of these speeds are very much gravity assisted and in level powered flight where they are fighting against gravity the Peregrine reaches 68mph/110kph and the Golden Eagle reaches 80mph/129kph, still fast but not the fastest. The fastest bird in powered level flight is a Swift (good name) but there is some debate as to which one! The White-throated Needletail Swift has been recorded at 105mph/169kph but there are claims of an Alpine Swift doing 110mph/177kph. It is not known whether either received points on their licence.

When it comes to running speed the fastest bird is the Ostrich with speeds of up to 43mph/70kph recorded, making the Ostrich the fastest thing on two legs. It could complete the 100m in just 5.14 seconds!

The larger birds of prey (or Raptors) are known for their wingspans*, the top five average wingspans for this fascinating group of birds is as follows:
1. Andean Condor 2.92metres
2. Himalayan Vulture 2.74metres
3. Californian Condor 2.74meters
4. Monk, or European Black, Vulture 2.72metres
5. Lappet-faced Vulture 2.69metres

The smallest wingspan of any raptor belongs to both the White-fronted Falconet and the Black-thighed Falconet both of which have a wingspan of 29cms.

The largest Raptor that actually kills its own prey as opposed to scavenging it depends on how you measure large (wingspan, length or weight). The three contenders are all Eagles and are the Harpy Eagle of South America, the Great Philippine Eagle and Steller's Fish Eagle, both of Asia. The largest Eagle of all time though was the Haast's Eagle of New Zealand which fed on Moas, it weighed in at around 14kgs and had a wingspan of up to 3metres. Once the Moas became extinct so did this mighty raptor.

With specially adapted dense bones and the clever trick of storing pebbles in their gizzard for extra ballast, the Penguins are the record holders when it comes to diving into the depths of the oceans. The undoubted champion is the Emperor Penguin which has been recorded at 565 metres below sea level.

*Wingspan measurements are controversial, many wingspans are taken from dried museum skins and these measurements tend to overestimate the wingspans considerably. Raptors in particular have had over estimated wingspans published and then repeated in subsequent books, the measurements shown here for this group of birds are taken from the excellent Raptors of the World by Ferguson-Lees and Christie which has tried to provide much more accurate measurements.

Survivors - Europe

Ringing birds leads to all sorts of data, one of the most popular databases is the longevity list; the amount of time that the bird has survived since it was first ringed up to its latest recovery. These are the top 50 of European ringing recoveries. Age is shown as years.months

Ranking	Species	Age
1st	Manx Shearwater	50.11
2nd	Tufted Duck	45.3
3rd	Fulmar	43.11
4th	Oystercatcher	43.4
5th	Guillemot	42.10
6th	Razorbill	42.0
7th	Pink-footed Goose	40.11
8th	Atlantic Puffin	40.10
9th	Grey Heron	37.6
10th	Gannet	37.5
11th	Eider Duck	36.10
12th	Wigeon	35.2
13th	Lesser Black-backed Gull	34.10
14th	Herring Gull	34.9
15th	Great Skua	34.6
16th	Common Gull	33.8
17th	Bar-tailed Godwit	33.1
18th	European Storm Petrel	33.0
19th	Common Tern	33.0
20th	Golden Eagle	32.0
21st	Curlew	31.10
22nd	Arctic Skua	31.1
23rd	Arctic Tern	30.11
24th	Leach's Storm Petrel	30.11
25th	Sandwich Tern	30.9

Ranking	Species	Age
26th	Black-headed Gull	30.7
27th	Common Shag	30.7
28th	Caspian Tern	30.0
29th	Black Guillemot	29.11
30th	White-tailed Eagle	29.10
31st	Great Black-backed Gull	29.2
32nd	Honey Buzzard	29.0
33rd	Mute Swan	28.10
34th	Brent Goose	28.10
35th	Dunlin	28.10
36th	Common Buzzard	28.9
37th	Kittiwake	28.6
38th	Barnacle Goose	28.2
39th	Black-throated Goose	27.10
40th	Avocet	27.10
41st	Brunnich's Guillemot	27.10
42nd	Greater Flamingo	27.6
43rd	Canada Goose	27.5
44th	Pintail Duck	27.5
45th	Eagle Owl	27.4
46th	Great Cormorant	27.2
47th	Redshank	26.11
48th	Osprey	26.11
49th	Knot	26.8
50th	Whooper Swan	26.6

*Source: European Union for Ringing - Euring

Survivors - America

Likewise here are the top 50 from American ringing (or banding as it is known in the states) recoveries. Age is shown as years.months.

Ranking	Species	Age
1st	Laysan Albatross	60.0
2nd	Gray-headed Albatross	47.2
3rd	Great Frigatebird	43.0
4th	Black-footed Albatross	42.1
5th	Sandhill Crane	36.7
6th	Black-browed Albatross	34.0
7th	Artic Tern	34.0
8th	Western Gull	33.11
9th	Sooty Tern	33.10
10th	Canada Goose	33.3
11th	Atlantic Puffin	33.1
12th	Bald Eagle	32.10
13th	Red-tailed Tropicbird	32.8
14th	Wandering Albatross	32.7
15th	Golden Eagle	31.7
16th	Mourning Dove	31.4
17th	Bonin Petrel	30.9
18th	Red-tailed Hawk	30.8
19th	Ashy Storm Petrel	30.0
20th	White Tern	29.9
21st	Caspian Tern	29.7
22nd	Brown Skua	28.10
23rd	Thick-billed Murre	28.8
24th	Whooping Crane	28.4
25th	Rhinoceros Auklet	28.3

Ranking	Species	Age
26th	Herring Gull	28.1
27th	California Gull	28.0
28th	Great Horned Owl	28.0
29th	Razorbill	28.0
30th	Royal Tern	28.0
31st	Brown Pelican	27.10
32nd	Mallard	27.7
33rd	Lesser Frigatebird	27.7
34th	Lesser Snow Goose	27.6
35th	Black Brant	27.6
36th	Ring-billed Gull	27.6
37th	Common Murre	27.1
38th	Red-legged Kittiwake	27.0
39th	Mute Swan	26.9
40th	American Black Duck	26.5
41st	Wedge-tailed Shearwater	26.3
42nd	Brown Booby	26.2
43rd	Gannet	26.1
44th	Black Guillemot	26.1
45th	Leach's Storm Petrel	26.0
46th	Gray-backed Tern	25.9
47th	Roseate Tern	25.8
48th	American Black Vulture	25.6
49th	Great Black-backed Gull	25.5
50th	Masked Booby	25.3

*Source: United States Geological Survey

Completely Cuckoo

Since the middle ages to be Cuckoo is to be a bit mad or crazy, since then the word has sprung the derivative Kooky which is often used to refer to someone who is a bit different. We also have Cloud Cuckoo Land which presumably is full of Cuckolded persons? The famous Roadrunner of the Looney Tunes Wile E. Coyote cartoons (*Beep Beep!*) is in fact a species of Cuckoo. Although it should be said that the Greater Roadrunner (the bird the cartoon was based on) doesn't look anything like the cartoon character.

The majority of species in the Cuckoo family are not actually brood parasites, they raise their own young. So it is possible to find a Cuckoo's nest! The European Cuckoo however is a brood parasite and will use a wide variety of species to rear its young for them. The following is a list of species that have been recorded as being used more than once in Europe.

Alpine Accentor	Aquatic Warbler	Barred Warbler
Bearded Tit	Black Redstart	Blackbird
Blackcap	Bluethroat	Brambling
Bullfinch	Chaffinch	Chiffchaff
Cirl Bunting	Corn Bunting	Crested Lark
Dartford Warbler	Dunnock	Firecrest
Garden Warbler	Goldcrest	Goldfinch
Golden Oriole	Grasshopper Warbler	Great Grey Shrike
Great Reed Warbler	Great Tit	Greenfinch
Grey Wagtail	Hawfinch	House Sparrow
Icterine Warbler	Lapland Bunting	Lesser Grey Shrike
Lesser Whitethroat	Linnet	Long-tailed Tit
Marsh Warbler	Meadow Pipit	Nightingale
Northern Wheatear	Ortolan Bunting	Orphean Warbler
Pied Flycatcher	Pied/White Wagtail	Red-backed Shrike
Redpoll	Redstart	Red-throated Pipit
Reed Bunting	Reed Warbler	Richard's Pipit

Ring Ouzel	Robin	Rock Pipit
Rock Thrush	Rustic Bunting	Sardinian Warbler
Sedge Warbler	Serin	Shore Lark
Short-toed Lark	Short-toed Treecreeper	Skylark
Song Thrush	Spotted Flycatcher	Starling
Stonechat	Swallow	Tawny Pipit
Thrush Nightingale	Treecreeper	Tree Sparrow
Tree Pipit	Twite	Whinchat
Whitethroat	Willow Warbler	Wood Warbler
Woodchat Shrike	Woodlark	Wren
Yellow Wagtail	Yellowhammer	

Currently in Britain the top three species used as hosts are the Dunnock, the Reed Warbler and the Meadow Pipit. The female Cuckoo has been known to visit up to 50 nests during the spring.

Caution – Not For Human Consumption

Other than the afore mentioned Pitohui there are very few birds that are poisonous to man. The others are the Blue-capped Ifrit, which like the Pitohui is also from Papua New Guinea where it too feeds on the toxically loaded Beetles that live there; the Little Shrikethrush, specimens of which have been shown to have toxic feathers as a result of their diet, again of poisonous beetles; The Spur-winged Goose of Africa can be fatal when eaten by humans if the birds have been eating Blister Beetles as they store the toxins from the beetles in their muscle tissue; and the Common Quail which can sometimes be poisonous at different stages of its migration depending on whether or not it has eaten an as yet unknown poisonous plant.

The Name Game

Before bird names became standardised many of our common birds had several different names depending on where in the UK you were from and also how old you were. Here is a list of some old/alternative names for birds found in the UK.

Modern Name	Old Name	Modern Name	Old Name
Avocet	Butterflip, Yelper	Barn Owl	Yellow Owl, White Owl, Billy Whit
Bittern	Bog Blutter, Moss Bummer	Blackbird	Merle, Amzel, Black Ouzel
Blackcap	Monk, Mock Nightingale	Black Guillemot	Puffinet, Greenland Dove
Blue Tit	Tom Tit, Tinnock, Billy Biter	Bullfinch	Nope, Budbird, Hoop
Chaffinch	Shell Apple, Taggy, Spink	Common Tern	Dip Pearl, Sea Swallow
Coot	Snyth, Bald Coot	Cormorant	Cole Goose, Parson
Corncrake	Land Rail, Daker Hen	Cuckoo	Gowk
Dipper	Water Crow, Water Ouzel	Dunnock	Blue Sparrow, Hedge Hatcher
Eider	St. Cuthbert's Duck	Fieldfare	Jack Bird, Felfit
Firecrest	Moonie	Fulmar	Mallimak
Great Grey Shrike	White Whisky John, Nine Killer	Great Skua	Bonxie, Tom Harry, Tod Bird
Greenfinch	Green Linnet, Green Bird	Greenshank	Green Legged Horseman
Green Woodpecker	Yaffle, Rain Bird, Woodwall	Goldcrest	Woodcock Pilot, Thumb Bird
Hoopoe	Dung Bird	House Martin	Eaves Swallow, Martin Swallow
House Sparrow	Spadger, Thatch Sparrow	Jackdaw	Daw, Jack, Kay
Jay	Jaypie	Kestrel	Windhover, Hover Hawk
Kingfisher	Halcyon,	Lapwing	Green Plover, Horny Wig, Peewit

Linnet	Grey Linnet, Red Linnet	Little Grebe	Dabchick, Small Ducker
Long-tailed Tit	Bottle Tit, Bum Barrel, Rose Muffin	Montagu's Harrier	Ash-coloured Falcon
Moorhen	Water Hen, Marsh Hen	Nightingale	Philomel
Nightjar	Goat Sucker, Fern Owl	Nuthatch	Nut Jobber, Mud Stopper
Osprey	Fish Hawk, Eagle Fisher	Oystercatcher	Seapie, Mussel Cracker
Pied Wagtail	Peggy Dishwasher	Pintail	Cracker, Sea Pheasant
Puffin	Sea Parrot, Sea Cockie	Raven	Corbie, Ralph
Red-backed Shrike	Murdering Pie, Wary Hanger	Red Kite	Crotchet-tailed Puttock, Gled
Redstart	Firetail, Branter	Ringed Plover	Sand Lark, Dull Willy, Stone Hatch
Robin	Ruddock, Bob, Redbreast	Skylark	Laverock
Smew	White Nun, Smee	Snipe	Mire Drummer, Heather Hammer
Song Thrush	Mavis, Throstle	Sparrowhawk	Hedge Hawk, Pigeon Hawk
Storm Petrel	Mother Carey's Chicken, Witch	Tawny Owl	Wood Owl, Jenny Owlet
Treecreeper	Bark Creeper, Tree Climber	Turnstone	Tangle Picker
Water Rail	Velvet Runner, Skitty	Whinchat	Ear Tick, Gorse Hatch
Whitethroat	Nettle Creeper, Straw Sucker	Woodpigeon	Cushat, Cow Prise
Wren	Jenny, Titty Todger, Two Fingers	Wryneck	Cuckoo's Mate, Snake Bird
Yellowhammer	Gold Spink, Scribbling Schoolmaster	Yellow Wagtail	Yellow Molly

The Manx Shearwater has the latin name of *Puffinus puffinus*. It's not a Puffin, it's not even an Auk. It is believed that the bird used to be called the Manks Puffin and that the name puffin refers to the cured carcasses of Shearwaters that were used as food hundreds of years ago. It was only much later that the actual Puffin started to be called a Puffin, probably because it too nests in burrows.

Alcatraz, as in the infamous ex prison, is Portuguese for Albatross but Spanish for Gannet. The word probably originates from the Arabic Al-cadous which means Pelican...

The Phalarope species, *Phalaropus fulicarius* was known as the Grey Phalarope in Britain and the Red Phalarope in America. In winter the birds plumage is Grey, hence the British name whilst in the summer the birds plumage is Red, hence the American name. To avoid further confusion the consensus is now to call the bird the Red Phalarope.

The Spanish name for the Lammergeier is very apt, Quebrantahuesos which literally means Bone Breaker.

It wasn't just the British that had all sorts of names for birds, here is a list of some old/alternative names for birds found in America.

Modern Name	Old Name	Modern Name	Old Name
American Bittern	Bog Pumper, Dunk a Doo	American Coot	Mudhen
American Goldfinch	Thistle Bird	American Kestrel	Sparrow Hawk
American Wigeon	Baldpate	American Woodcock	Bog Sucker
Bar-tailed Godwit	White-rumped Godwit	Barn Owl	Monkey-faced Owl
Bermuda Petrel	Cahow	Black-bellied Plover	Bullhead
Black-footed Albatross	Black Gooney Bird	Black-necked Stilt	Lawyer
Black Vulture	Carrion Crow	Brown Booby	Brewster's Booby
Bufflehead	Butterball	Canada Goose	Honker
Cattle Egret	Buff-backed Heron	Cedar Waxwing	Cherry-bird

Modern Name	Old Name	Modern Name	Old Name
Chuck-wills-widow	Twixt hell and the White Oak	Common Cuckoo	Khasia Hills Cuckoo
Common Tern	Sea Swallow	Cooper's Hawk	Big Blue Darter
Dunlin	Purre	Gadwall	Gray Duck
Gannet	Solan Goose	Goldeneye	Cobhead
Great Blue Heron	Blue Crane	Greater Roadrunner	Chaparral Cock
Greater Scaup	Greater Blackhead	Green-backed Heron	Fly-up-the-creek, Shite Poke
Grey Crowned Yellowthroat	Ground Chat	Hooded Merganser	Cock Robin
Horned Grebe	Hell Diver	House Finch	Burrion
Kingbird	Tyrant Flycatcher	Knot	Robin Snipe, Grayback
Lesser Scaup	Lesser Blackhead	Lesser Yellowlegs	Lesser Tatler
Mallard	Green-headed Duck	Merlin	Pigeon Hawk
Northern Flicker	Gilded Flicker	Northern Shoveler	Spoonbill
Peregrine	Peale's Falcon, Duck Hawk	Philadelphia Vireo	Brotherly-love Greenlet
Pileated Woodpecker	Log Cock	Red-breasted Merganser	Fish Duck
Red-tailed Hawk	Cooper's Buzzard	Ruddy Duck	Sleepy Duck
Ruddy Turnstone	Calico Black	Rufous-sided Towhee	Chewink
Sabine's Gull	Fork-tailed Gull	Sage Grouse	Cock of the Plains
Sandhill Crane	Little Brown Crane	Sharp-shinned Hawk	Little Blue Darter
Short-billed Dowitcher	Brownback	Short-tailed Shearwater	Mutton Bird
Siberian Tit	Alaska Chickadee	Snow Bunting	Snowflake
Sooty Shearwater	Black Hagdon	Sora	Ortolan
Water Pipit	Brownback	Whimbrel	Hudsonian Curlew
White-tailed Eagle	Gray Sea Eagle	Whooping Crane	White Crane
Wood Duck	Acorn Duck	Yellow-billed Cuckoo	California Cuckoo

Of birds and men

European Robins are well known gardener companions following the human gardener closely ready to pounce on any juicy worm or other invertebrate that is inadvertently dug up during weeding, planting etc. It is likely that this behaviour is an adaptation from their behaviour of following Wild Boar as they root through woodland leaf litter and soils looking for food. Whilst you may think that the Robin in your flowerbed is cute, the Robin just thinks you are a Pig!

Penduline Tits make amazing nests, hanging domes suspended on thin twigs above water. In Africa the nests are much admired and many species have their nests stolen to be used as purses by people.

The Stephen Island Wren of New Zealand became known to science when one was killed and brought home by the island's lighthouse keeper's cat. Within a few months of becoming known to science it was extinct. Predated out of existence by the several cats present and by the lighthouse keeper who readily sold specimens to collectors throughout the world.

The record for the longest continuous satellite tracking of a bird is held by a White Stork. It was tracked for 2,033 days before the bird flew into an electrical pylon and was electrocuted.

Electrical pylons can be a serious hazard for many larger bird species. The Spanish Imperial Eagle is one of the rarest Eagle species in the world with a total of 380 pairs recorded in 2012. In some years as many as 30% of newly fledged Spanish Imperial Eagles are killed by hitting pylons.

Normally when Bird and Man clash the bird comes off worst. However, if the man happens to be in Northern Queensland in Australia it might just be the other way around. The Cassowary is a serious bird that also has a serious attitude, standing at just under 2 metres tall and weighing in at over 80kgs they are an adversary that you want to avoid especially as each foot has a 12cm long, sharply spiked, claw just perfect for disembowelling... In a 6 year period over 150 people were 'mugged' by Cassowaries in Northern Queensland, six of them receiving serious injuries. Don't think that having a dog will help you either as 35 dogs were also injured during the same period.

It has been estimated that over 100 million birds die each year in the United States following collisions with glass windows.

It is estimated that domestic cats in Britain kill as many as 65 million birds a year. In the US the number of birds killed by domestic cats is estimated at 3.7 billion! Yet for some reason birdwatchers still keep cats as pets – why?

Birds of prey are now regular in cities throughout the world. These artificial environments can hold large numbers of prey items for them to exploit, especially feral pigeons. However this isn't necessarily a win win situation for the birds of prey. Cooper's Hawk in America has readily taken to cities and the resident pigeons. Due to the abundance of food the Hawks in the cities breed earlier and lay more eggs than the hawks in the countryside but over 50% of the chicks are likely to die before leaving the nest due to a disease that the pigeons carry called Avian Trichomoniasis. Proving there really is no such thing as a Free Lunch.

The House Sparrow was introduced into New York city in 1852 to help control 'tree worms'. It is now one of the most abundant birds in North America. No one knows what impact this has had on the native wildlife.

Ecotourism should be a good thing for birds. Unfortunately this isn't always the case. At least two studies have shown that it can have a negative affect on some species. The Hoatzin of the Amazonian basin is a favourite 'tick' for many bird watching eco-tourists. However it has been found that chicks in areas where tourists visit have a lower survival rate than chicks in areas with no tourist visits. It has been speculated that the very presence of a large group of people causes stress for the adults and affects their behaviour reducing the number of feeding visits made to the chicks. This is certainly the case with the Yellow-eyed Penguin of New Zealand. When tourists are visiting their nesting colonies the adults delay going to the nest with food which means the chicks in these areas get less food to eat. Fledglings in areas subject to high numbers of tourists weigh less than those from areas without tourism. Lower fledgling weight is extremely likely to have a negative affect on their survival chances.

In September 2013 an Egyptian fisherman carried out a citizens arrest on an alleged spy. The spy was a White Stork passing through Egypt on migration. The fisherman had become suspicious of the Stork due to a mysterious device fitted to its back that had perhaps been fitted by a sinister foreign power for espionage purposes... On delivery to the local police – where the bird was locked up in a cell - a local vet soon identified the device as being a tracking device used by French scientists studying migratory behaviour. Although this proved the bird's innocence the poor Stork was detained for several more hours whilst prosecutors debated whether or not it had a case to answer!

eanwhile in 2011 a Griffon Vulture was arrested in Sudan for spying for Israel. The rd was captured red handed carrying GPS equipment and marked with tags from el Aviv University, obviously just a cover name for Mossad. Again the bird was part a migration study.

ne Tel Aviv University (or should that be Mossad?) ringing program has more cently caused problems for a Kestrel that was arrested in Turkey and accused of oying for the Israelis. The bird was eventually declared innocent and released but ot before it was medically examined with x rays to ensure it wasn't harbouring any ophisticated espionage equipment.

he above cases may at first glance seem like examples of human paranoia but rds have indeed been used for espionage purposes. Domestic Pigeons were fitted ith cameras by the German military prior to World War 1 to photograph eighbouring countries and in the conflict itself they were used by Allies to notograph troop movements during the battles of Verdun and the Somme but the esults weren't very satisfactory. The CIA acknowledge the use of pigeons fitted with ameras in the 1970s but won't reveal details of their missions. The next time you re out birdwatching you might want to consider who is watching you.

n a related military theme Turkeys were used as parachutes during the Spanish ivil War. Nationalist fighters besieged in a monastery in Andalucía had delicate nedical supplies delivered to them by Turkeys who had the goods strapped to their odies. Released from a plane above the site they gently flapped their wings as they escended ensuring that the medical supplies had a soft landing. Unfortunately for ne birds they were also a convenient food package. Edible parachutes.

A little bird told me...

The English language is dotted with all sorts of phrases, idioms and proverbs that make reference to birds in various contexts. If you listen out for them you will be amazed how many you will hear in a day, whether in general conversation, on the radio, on the television etc. Below is a list of just some of the many. Why not have a go at Bird Phrase Bingo and see if you can tick off 10 of them in a day? You may find that you take to it like a duck to water...

As bald as a Coot		Swan song	
In fine feather		Sick as a parrot	
Chicken out		Eagle eyed	
As the Crow flies		Not a dicky bird	
The Birds and the bees		Birds eye view	
Out for a Duck		Goose bumps	
Cat amongst the Pigeons		Pecking order	
S/he's no spring Chicken		A nest egg	
Clip someone's wings		Dead as a Dodo	
Cold Turkey		Night Owl	
Pigeon hole		Ruffled his/her feathers	
Wild Goose chase		Hen pecked	
The early bird catches the worm		Rule the roost	
Lovey Dovey		Kill two birds with one stone	
Free as a bird		Sitting Duck	
One Swallow doesn't make a summer		Don't count your Chickens before they hatch	

Body parts

When you pull the wishbone of your Sunday roast you are actually breaking the bird's collarbones/clavicles.

The flight (breast) muscles of flying birds usually account for 25% of its total body weight. In some species of Pigeon though it is almost 40%.

The beaks of Blackbirds, Mallards and Zebra Finches all glow in ultraviolet light.

Captive Geese have hearts and livers that weigh less than wild Geese. Their intestines are also shorter in length.

Birds just have one body opening, called the cloaca, for urine, faeces, sperm and eggs to pass through. In most species of birds the males don't have a penis.

Male Sungrebes that live in Central and South America have the unique ability to carry their young under their wings when flying. They have pouches of skin under the wing and are able to grip the chicks firmly in them ensuring that they don't fall out on the journey.

The Common Starling of Europe has an arrangement of muscles that enable it to push their beaks into the ground and then open the gape so that they can then look down through to see if there are any juicy grubs to grab and eat.

Gannets and the closely related Boobies dive from a great height into the sea. To protect them from the impact they have air sacs between the skin and muscles in their face and chest acting almost like bubble wrap cushioning the blow.

To conserve energy and minimise weight the reproductive organs of most birds are shrunk down and kept as small as possible. However, in the breeding season they increase in size rapidly and in some cases spectacularly. Some species of Quail have testicles that increase in size by 400 times in just a few weeks!

But not all birds stop at shrinking their reproductive organs. Waders can shrink their internal organs including their brains so that they have more 'space' to store fat ahead of their long distance migrations.

The Sword-billed Hummingbird of South America is the only species of bird whose bill is longer than its body.

Some birds such as the White Stork will defecate/urinate on to their legs as a way of cooling themselves down. As the fluids evaporate off the legs it produces a cooling effect that helps cool the blood vessels below the scaly skin of the legs. The process is called Urohidrosis.

Other birds use their excreta differently. Both the Hoopoe and the Fieldfare use it as a defensive weapon. If a predator, or an overly keen birdwatcher, approaches the nest hole of a Hoopoe too closely the young birds within it will spray their excreta in well aimed jets at them. In case this isn't enough they also produce a foul smelling oil making the nest absolutely stink. In the Fieldfare it is the adults that take the initiative, they will quite literally bomb any predator that comes too close to their nests with their excreta. The results for the predator can be extremely serious, particular avian predators. There have been several recorded instances of Kestrels dying as a result of having their feathers completely clogged with Fieldfare poo.

Unlike us mammals birds generally need to conserve water. As a result they don't urinate in the same way as mammals – mixing the uric acid with copious amounts of water – instead they expel uric acid in a crystalline form which is the distinctive white splat that is seen in bird droppings. So if a bird leaves a nice white splat on your favourite jacket it's not actually poo but wee. Not sure if that makes it any better though!

Because the uric acid is not diluted with water it is very concentrated with various nitrates. In the past large industries grew up around large sea bird colonies where the droppings (guano) were harvested and processed. Initially they were used to make saltpetre (Potassium Nitrate) for gunpowder production and later on they were used for fertilizer production.

The different parts of a birds body have been given names, many of which we use to describe other animals and ourselves, so you will be familiar with many of them such as head and tail. But there are other terms that you might not be so familiar with, such as supercilium and alula. The following pages take you through the various parts of birds and show you just exactly what bit is called what. So the next time you hear someone talking about crown stripes you'll know they aren't talking about a new paint...

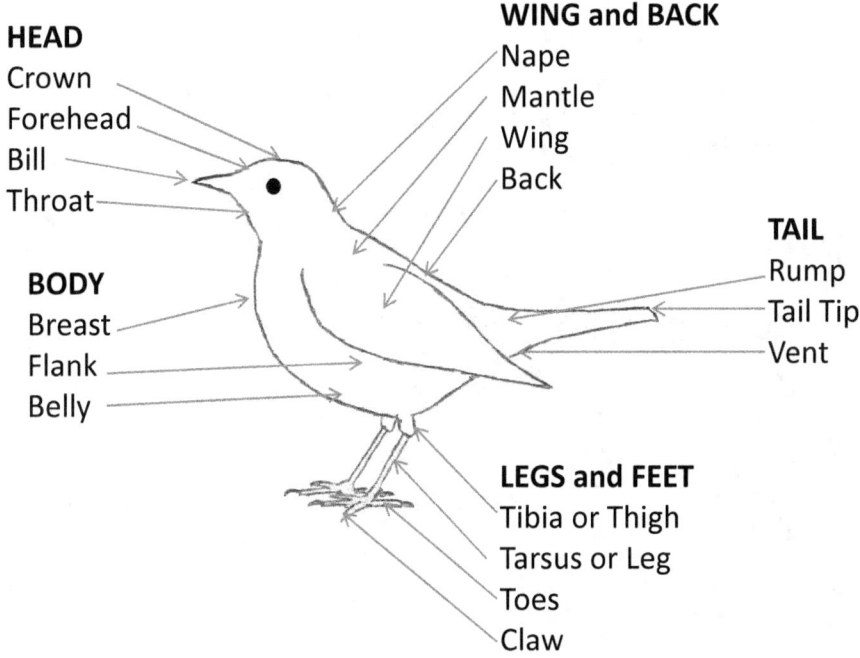

WING and BACK
Nape
Mantle
Wing
Back

HEAD
Crown
Forehead
Bill
Throat

TAIL
Rump
Tail Tip
Vent

BODY
Breast
Flank
Belly

LEGS and FEET
Tibia or Thigh
Tarsus or Leg
Toes
Claw

The heads of birds are often intricately marked and can be key to the birds identification. This head is of a made up bird but it shows many of the features that can be found complete with their names.

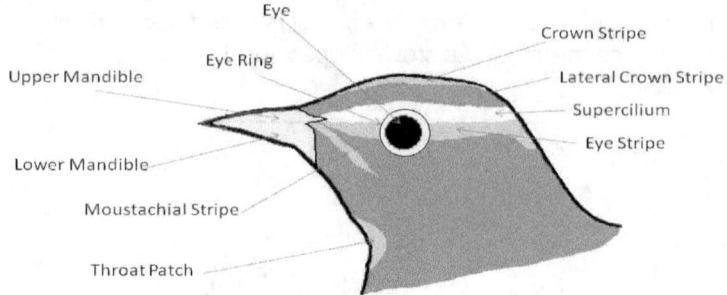

The feathers of a birds wing are given their own names with the different feathers performing different functions. The names for these groups of feathers are shown below on an imaginary wing.

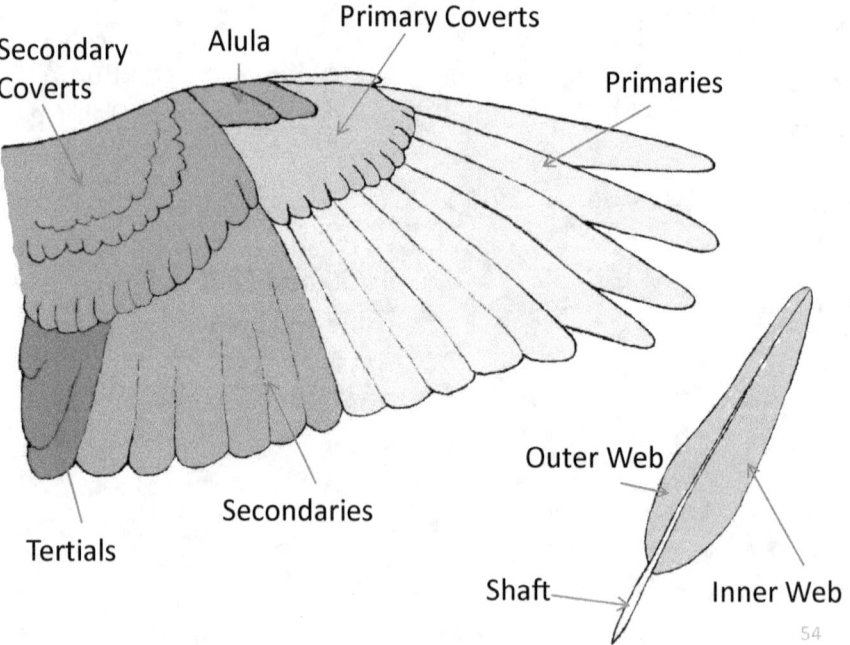

In flight the tail shape of birds can be useful in helping to identify the species, especially when they are silhouetted against a bright sky making it hard to see any markings, below are 6 tail shapes that you may see. The proportions of a flying bird can be useful in identification too, this is particularly important when identifying birds of prey, shown below are the parts to check out when looking at their proportions. Finally birds of prey often have distinctive markings when seen from below and when seen from above (when looking down a valley for example) and these body markings can again be very useful things to know.

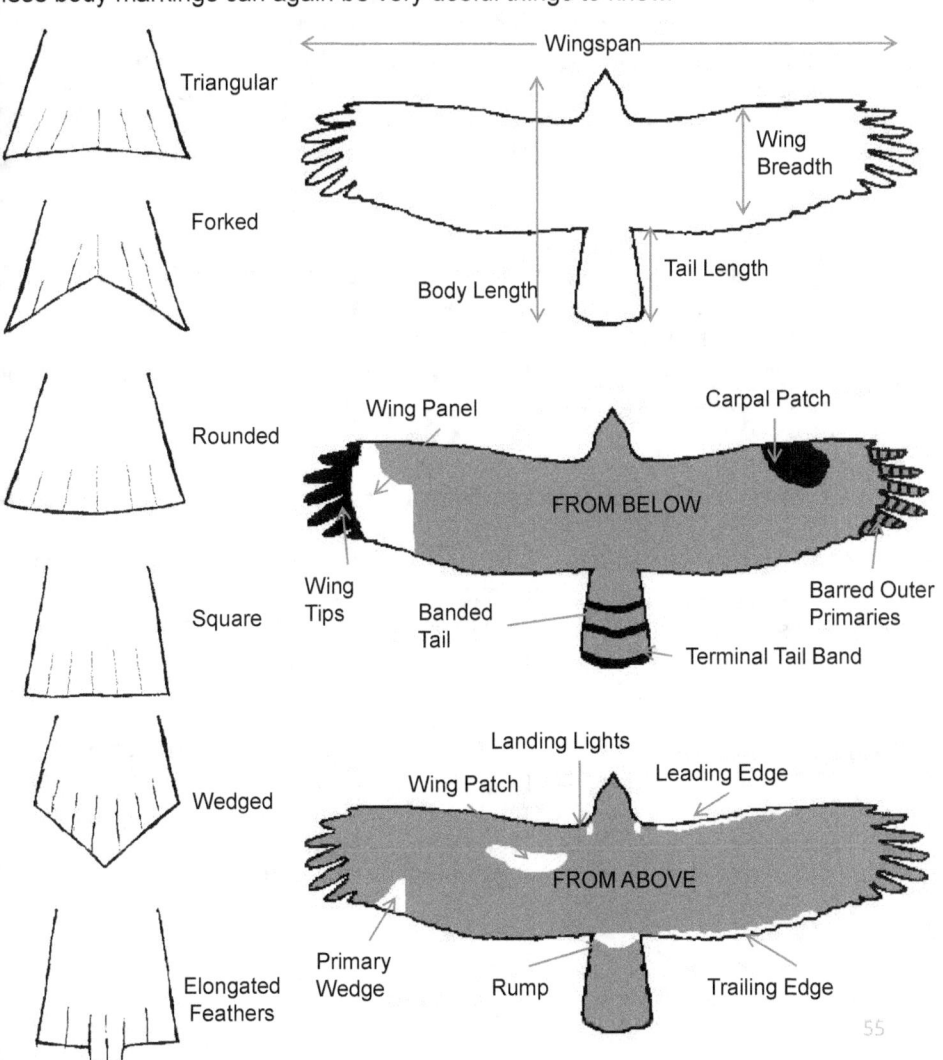

Triangular

Forked

Rounded

Square

Wedged

Elongated Feathers

Wingspan

Wing Breadth

Tail Length

Body Length

Wing Panel

Carpal Patch

FROM BELOW

Wing Tips

Banded Tail

Barred Outer Primaries

Terminal Tail Band

Landing Lights

Wing Patch

Leading Edge

FROM ABOVE

Primary Wedge

Rump

Trailing Edge

Sound and Vision

Birds, unlike most mammals and some humans, including me, have perfect colour vision.

Many birds are able to see in the Ultraviolet spectrum. The Common Kestrel of Europe uses this ability when hunting. Kestrels eat Voles and Voles use regular runs that often criss-cross grassy areas forming networks. As they go along their runs Voles urinate and defecate, unfortunately for the Voles their waste products reflect UV light making their runs visible to the Kestrels. When you see a Kestrel hovering over an area of rough grass it's likely to be hovering over a heavily used junction of Vole runs just waiting for lunch to come trundling along the 'glowing' trail.

The ears of many Owls, such as the Barn Owl, are adapted so that they can accurately pinpoint their prey even when it is hidden beneath vegetation or snow. Not only is one ear bigger than the other but they are also positioned differently on the sides of the head, with one being higher up than the other. The species of Owl that rely heavily on sound when hunting have characteristic disc shaped faces that help direct the sound waves to the ears.

The raptors and other birds including Kingfishers and Swallows have two light sensitive areas (fovea) on their retinas giving them much greater visual acuity than birds that just have one. The Kingfisher uses its second fovea when it enters the water enabling it to see its prey clearly beneath the surface. Swallows use both their fovea when hunting small flying insects on the wing at speed, they have large brains for their body size and these are needed to process the information from the eyes ensuring that the Swallow gets its meal and avoids colliding with any objects.

The eyes of many of the larger Eagles are the same size as human eyes even though the birds are much smaller than us. Their vision is much better than ours, raptors have a much greater concentration of light gathering colour sensitive cells (Cones) in their eyes than we do or indeed any other vertebrate. It has been demonstrated that some Eagles can see a Rabbit up to a mile away (1.6km). Hence the saying 'Eagle eyed'.

Owls have very large eyes, as a result the eyes are fixed in position in the head and cannot be moved, so instead of moving their eyes to look at something they swivel their heads around to look at it. They can swivel their heads through a radius of 270 degrees making it very easy for them to see behind them without having to move their bodies at all. This also has the advantage of reducing any sound when watching potential prey from a perch.

The American Woodcock's eyes are placed on the side of their heads in such a way that they have 360 degree all round vision, in other words they can see what is going on even directly behind them. No other bird is believed to have this large a field of vision.

The song of a male Bittern is called a 'Boom'. This is a good name for it as it can be heard up to 3 miles/ 4.8kilometres away.

Us mammals make sound via our larynx whilst birds makes theirs via a very different structure called the syrinx. Whilst they serve the same purpose the mammal larynx is totally inefficient (although it functions well enough for us) when compared to the birds syrinx. Generally speaking the larynx converts less than 5% of the energy generated by forcing air through it in to sound whilst the syrinx converts almost 100% of it into sound.

The Chaffinch, a common resident throughout Europe, will alter the way it sings if singing in a noisy environment – next to fast flowing rivers or beside busy roads for example. The bird will continually repeat the phrases in its song to make sure it gets heard and understood by other rival chaffinches that may be nearby.

The first known recording of bird song was made way back in 1889 by Ludwig Koch who eventually ended up helping to establish the BBC's natural history sounds library.

Human noise, especially in urban environments is known to have an effect on birdsong. Species such as Blue Tits and Great Tits all start singing earlier in cities than in the countryside and it is thought that this may be because they are avoiding competing with the morning noise of the human population waking up and going to work, school, etc. Great Tits have been shown to increase the volume and pitch of their song in urban areas to try and combat the background noise which may otherwise drown them out.

The Oilbirds of South America, relatives of the Nightjars, are nocturnal in their habits. Although there are lots of nocturnal birds the Oilbird is the only one that feeds on fruit, all the others feed on insects or are predators. The Oilbird uses an audible call as a type of sonar when it is navigating through the cave systems in which it lives. The sounds bounce back off the walls of the cave and the bird is able to interpret these echoes and thus avoid crashing.

Many of our familiar song birds are widely distributed over a large geographical area, within this area some populations develop an 'accent' to their songs. They still sing the same song as one another but it sounds, even to our hearing, slightly different.

In Great Britain the Blackbird is the early bird. Normally it is the first bird to start singing in the dawn chorus closely followed by the Robin.

The Feather Flight Touch

The feather evolved during the time of the dinosaurs, indeed it is now widely accepted that birds evolved from the dinosaurs themselves. However, the first creatures to have feathers were not birds but were dinosaurs and these feathers were not for flight but probably for thermo regulation or, if you like, for keeping warm.

Humans long ago realised that feathers were very useful for keeping warm too and have used them in bedding materials and clothing stuffed with feathers ever since.

The word Pen comes from the latin *Penna* which means feather. Large flight feathers were used as pens, called quills for hundreds of years before the invention of more typical pens in the 1800s. Documents such as the Magna Carta and the American Declaration of Independence were all written using feathers.

All of the flightless birds in the world evolved from flying birds.

Other than when raising their young the Common Swift is a full time flyer, it feeds, mates and even sleeps on the wing. It is believed to be the bird that spends the most time flying. As a result its feet and legs are virtually redundant and are much reduced in size. A Swift on level ground would be totally hopeless as it would not be able to walk or run. The Latin name for Swift is *Apus* which literally means no foot.

To fly, a bird needs to make itself as light as possible. But some flying birds also swim underwater when being as light as possible isn't that helpful. Cormorants and Anhingas (sometimes known as snakebirds) are unusal in the bird world in that they don't have a preen gland and therefore they don't waterproof their flight feathers. As soon as the flight feathers come in contact with the water they become totally waterlogged and therefore heavy helping the bird hunt for fish under the surface. Because of the lack of preen gland Cormorants and Anhingas have to dry themselves off after a swim and that is what they are doing when they stand on a rock with their wings held out in the sun. The Grebes on the other hand do have a preen gland but are able to compress their feathers tight in very close to their bodies squeezing all the air out of them just as they dive.

It is well known that the Ptarmigan (also known as the Rock Ptarmigan), a grouse of the northern latitudes, turns white in the winter to blend in with the snow. But they also have other highly specialised feather adaptations to help them in the harsh winters as well. Their nostrils are feathered to help filter the cold air and their feet are also feathered to help them walk across fresh snow.

The Phalaropes are a dainty species of bird that uses its feathers to trap air enabling them to float with ease. In fact they trap so much air that they literally bob along the surface and can easily be blown about by wind.

The Emperor Penguin has the highest density of feathers of any bird, about 15 per square centimetre. These trap air and act as a very efficient insulator but then, lets face it, they need good insulation bearing in mind they stand on ice in temperatures as low as -40 C...

The feathers of Owls are specially adapted to give them silent flight. The flight feathers have a soft 'fringing' to them which muffles the sound of their wings in the air enabling them to catch their sharp eared prey by surprise.

Sandgrouse have several feather adaptations to help them survive in the harsh arid environment in which they live. They have a very dense layer of under feathers which helps protect them from the hot baking sun in the day time but also can then be used to keep them warm in the cold of the desert night. Water in the environment in which Sandgrouse live is a precious commodity and birds often have to fly long distances to obtain it. Their young however need water and can't fly but the Sandgrouse have solved this problem by having specially adapted feathers on their belly that absorb and then retain the water in them even during flight. The birds are able to carry as much as 20ml of water back to their thirsty chicks each time.

The Hummingbirds are supreme flyers, beating their wings in horizontal figures of 8 just like a Dragonfly. Like the Dragonfly they can also carry out very precise movements, moving up, down, sideways, forwards and backwards all just by slightly varying their wing movements. Some Hummingbird species can beat their wings 200 times per second.

Many seed eating birds keep pieces of grit in their gizzards to help grind their food but for small flying birds this brings additional weight. The Bearded Reedling (also known as the Bearded Tit) is a particularly small flying bird whose diet varies depending on the season. During the winter it feeds on seeds and needs the grit in its gizzard to grind them, but when spring comes it switches to insects and when it does this it gets rid of its grit to keep its weight down, enabling it to be more nimble in flight which is an obvious advantage when catching insects.

On the Move

Approximately 20% of all bird species migrate. Whilst we associate migration with large flocks of birds flying overhead not all migrations are undertaken in flight. Some species of Penguin migrate by swimming, often over distances of several hundred miles, whilst the Emu will walk vast distances in search of rains and therefore food, much like the famed Wildebeest of Africa. The Guillemot (or Common Murre) also swims on migration, once the chicks are big enough to, quite literally, tumble off their nest ledge into the sea, the adults start to moult their flight feathers all at once and are therefore flightless for about 8 weeks. During this period they migrate by swimming over hundreds of miles.

The Arctic Tern is *the* long distance traveller of the birds. They breed in the north, some of them right up in the Arctic Circle, during the northern hemisphere summer. They then migrate all the way down to the Antarctic to spend the southern hemisphere summer there. This is a round trip of between 21,750 miles/35,000 kilometres and 24,850 miles/40,000 kilometres, far more than your average motorist does in a year. An Arctic Tern that was ringed in America and recovered 34 years later had potentially flown 845,000 miles/1,360,000kilometres just on migration flights alone – that's a lot of miles on the clock!

Because the Arctic Tern spends its year enjoying both the summers of the northern and southern hemispheres it has been suggested that they spend the highest percentage of their lives in daylight of any living creature.

"Sod all that flying!"

Migration is tough and exacts a heavy toll but the rewards are worth it or the bird wouldn't do it. The Barn Swallow suffers a 20% mortality rate on every migration. For the young, embarking on their first migration flight (which incidentally they do without parental supervision as the adults migrate before the young) suffer as much as 50% mortality on that first migration.

As mentioned before Emus embark on walking migrations, generally walking at a steady 4.5mph/7kph and covering distances of up to 300 miles/500 kilometres. When doing so they can lose up to half of their bodyweight.

Whilst on migration (and also when roosting) Hummingbirds have to slow their kidney's metabolic processes right down to stop themselves literally peeing to death! They ingest huge amounts of water from the nectar that they feed on and have to excrete this excess fluid continuously. But when unable to feed whilst flying across sea on migration they have to reduce the kidneys metabolic rate otherwise they would dehydrate and die.

The directional finding ability of birds is extraordinary especially when compared to our own! Migration tests this ability to its limits but it is not just in migration that birds use this ability. The Wandering Albatross of the South Atlantic is a great example. It breeds on small islands, often not much more than a lump of rock jutting up out of the sea. Yet, even after feeding flights of thousands of kilometres over a completely featureless open sea , it can find its nest. No one really knows how they do this but one thing for certain is that the Wandering Albatross doesn't just wander, it knows exactly where it is going. Now that's a real wonder.

Widely Spread

The most naturally widespread of the bird families is the Procellaridae (Fulmars, Petrels and Shearwaters etc). Members of the family can be found in all the latitudes of the globe, quite literally from pole to pole.

The Roseate Tern, the Caspian Tern, the Barn Owl and the Osprey are among the mostly widely distributed bird species on the planet. But the bird with the largest natural breeding range is the Peregrine Falcon. The only large non polar land mass that doesn't have Peregrines is New Zealand.

The House Sparrow, thanks to the help of Humans who have repeatedly introduced it throughout all parts of the world, is the most widely distributed species on the planet.

A Question of Identity

The males and the females of the Eclectus Parrot of New Guinea and Australia are so different from one another that up to the early part of the 20th Century they were considered as being separate species. Sexual dimorphism in parrots isn't a common trait and with the male being a bright emerald green and the female being a bright red and purple/blue bird you can understand how people would get confused. Luckily the birds weren't confused.

Brewster's Warbler in the eastern USA is a fertile hybrid produced when the closely related Golden-winged Warbler and Blue-winged Warbler interbreed with one another. Normally Brewster's Warblers breed with other Brewster's Warblers to produce yet more Brewster's Warblers but occasionally they will breed with either a Blue-winged or Golden-winged Warbler to produce another fertile and viable hybrid called Lawrence's Warbler. Hope you followed that.

The Gouldian Finch, an endemic bird of Australia, normally has a black head. However, around about 25% of birds have a red head instead. Just to confuse things further every now and then a yellow headed one turns up as well.

The Herring Gull and Lesser Black-backed Gull of Britain are good examples of bird clines. When a bird has a large distribution covering many areas there tends to be some variation from one area to the next. Birds in area 1 are slightly different from birds in area 2 whilst birds in area 3 are slightly different from the area 2 birds but more different from the area 1 birds and so on and so on depending on how many areas a birds population covers. The populations in these areas are called Clines. Clines can and do interbreed but if the number of clines is large enough that it eventually covers around the world then it is possible that the birds at either end of the cline are so different from one another that they either cannot, or do not, interbreed. As it happens the two ends of a Gull cline meet in Britain, one of these clines is the Herring Gull whilst the other is the Lesser Black-backed Gull. The two are so different from one another that they don't (there are always exceptions) interbreed and thus form separate species.

In October 2012 a new species for Britain turned up in Dorset, the problem is no one really knows whether it was a Pale-legged Leaf Warbler or a Sakhalin Leaf Warbler. The two species are so alike that it is virtually impossible to identify them without genetic analysis or by hearing their song. Unfortunately like so many lost vagrants the bird didn't sing and vanished very quickly meaning that the new species for Britain is likely to remain as an either/or.

Miscellaneous miscellany

In America there is an industry that makes cowboy hats and belts out of the skins of Turkeys.

The Emu can't walk backwards, something it shares with its fellow Australian the Kangaroo. Both animals feature on the country's coat of arms as a symbol for progression, ie only moving forwards.

The Emu may not be able to walk backwards but only one group of birds are able to fly backwards – the Hummingbirds.

In Nordic folklore Flokki dicovered Iceland by using a Raven.

The Great Spotted Woodpecker of Europe 'drums' on dead wood in trees to signal its presence during the breeding season. When doing so it strikes its bill against the tree up to 20 times a second.

The male Greater Rhea looks after its young instead of the female bird. When doing so it will defend its young from all comers including other Rheas, Humans and predators. There is even a report of a male trying to attack an airplane! Whilst Greater Rhea are a South American bird there is now a well established breeding population in Germany that formed when three pairs escaped from a farm in 2000, there are now thought to be over 120 birds living wild.

A Common Swift was ringed as a chick in its nest and recovered 18 years later, it has been estimated that it had probably flown over 4,000,000miles/6,440,000 kilometres since it left its nest.

Eleven out of the Seventeen species of Penguin are not found in the Antarctic, indeed most Penguin species are unlikely to ever see ice. Penguins are thought to have evolved in a tropical climate.

Laboratory tests have demonstrated that Feral Pigeons can be trained to distinguish between paintings by Claude Monet and paintings by Pablo Picasso. They are able to recognise the different styles of the two artists. Why scientists needed to find this out is not known...

"Personally I prefer his Blue period"

When the American politician Dick Cheney was the vice-president of the United States he shot and wounded his lawyer whilst out on a hunting trip. Apparently he mistook his lawyer for a Bobwhite Quail, well that's what he told his lawyer...

The Ancient Egyptians not only mummified their Pharaohs but also birds such as Falcons, Ibis and Hawks.

On a similar theme to the Feral Pigeon science experiment, Java Sparrows have been the subject of studies to ascertain their musical preferences. When given the choice between Johann Sebastian Bach or the more modern Arnold Schoenberg they would chose music by Bach. When the experiment was repeated with Antonio Vivaldi and the more modern Elliot Carter they would chose music by Vivaldi. It would seem that Java Sparrows prefer old school classical music over more modern versions. The world is a much better place thanks to this pioneering scientific work!

Many trivia books state that ducks' quacks don't echo. This is a complete fallacy of course. A quack like any other sound is a 'wave' that will rebound off solid objects creating an echo effect. Where the myth of non echoing quacks originates is a mystery but perhaps Pliny studied ducks after the Ostrich...

The symbol of the United States is of course the Bald Eagle. However, the founding father Benjamin Franklin wanted it to be the Wild Turkey.

Other than the odd human explorer, Skuas venture closer to the South Pole than any other vertebrate.

Britain's only endemic bird is the Scottish Crossbill

The Kea, a Parrot from New Zealand is a bit of a delinquent. They have been charged with various crimes including criminal damage and burglary. They have the unfortunate habit of stripping wiper blades off cars as well as removing the rubber seal around windscreens. They will enter houses via open windows and doors to steal food, if these are all locked tight they have even been known to enter the house via the chimney to get something to eat. When they will learn to open fridges is not known.

Over half of all bird species belong to the Passerines (which means perching birds), this order is widespread throughout the world and is very diverse. The largest Passerine is the Common Raven of the northern hemisphere whilst the smallest is the Short-tailed Pygmy Tyrant of South America.

In Europe, the 10 millionth ringed bird recovery was a Barn Swallow, originally rung in Malta it was recovered alive in the Czech Republic in 2011.

Small birds will lose up to 10% of their bodyweight overnight.

Prions are small members of the Petrel family. They have an excellent sense of smell and are able to distinguish their mates from other Prions in pitch darkness just by their scent.

The words Auspicious and Augury (as in it doesn't augur well) have their roots in the Roman word Auspex which means 'lookers at birds' or quite simply Birdwatchers. The name refered to people who used to predict the future by interpreting the flight of birds.

The Archaeopteryx is widely thought to be the earliest known example of a bird. However, in China in 2013, a new earlier species was discovered called Aurornis xui. It is believed, but not yet finally proven, that the fossil dates from 10 million years before that of the Archaeopteryx.

A breeding colony of Penguins is called a Rookery.

Many birds will use carotenoid pigments that are found in their food to produce bright plumage colours – think Pink Flamingos. However, Parrots are able to synthesise their own colour pigments all by themselves making them unique in the animal world.

Potoos and Nightjars are closely related bird families. Both are active nocturnally and spend the days roosting. To protect them from predators they are superbly camouflaged. If a potential predator approaches near to a European Nightjar it will squint its eyes. In this way it can still keep an eye on the predator but doesn't compromise its camouflage by having its large dark eye wide open – something a predator may well spot. Potoos have taken this a step further and have a notch in their upper eyelid so that they can monitor any threats whilst their eyes are actually shut.

The largest Pigeon in the world is the Victoria Crowned Pigeon of New Guinea, it weighs in at 2.4kgs although some have been recorded as being 3.5kgs. The title of the largest pigeon once belonged to the Dodo so perhaps it's not a great title to hold, indeed the Victoria Crowned Pigeon is listed as Vulnerable by the world conservation body the IUCN.

Parrots are the most variably sized bird order in the world. The smallest parrot is the Buff-faced Pygmy Parrot of New Guinea, it weighs just 10gms and measures about 8.5cms in length. The longest Parrot is the Hyacinth Macaw measuring 100cms in length whilst the heaviest is the flightless Kakapo of New Zealand that can weigh up to 4kgs, that's 400 times heavier than the Buff-faced Pygmy.

Hoatzins are odd birds in many ways, looking something like a chicken crossed with a pheasant they live in trees that line the rivers of the Amazon basin. In the first 8 weeks of their lives they have 2 hooked claws on their wings that they use to climb about the trees that they live in. If startled they drop like a stone out of the tree and down into the river below. Young Hoatzins can swim, soon reaching the bank again and then using their claws to clamber up through the branches to get back to their perch.

It used to be believed that Hummingbirds migrated on the backs of Canada Geese. Absolute rubbish of course but what a great image!

Generally speaking birds live longer than similar sized mammals.

The Fork-tailed Drongo learns the alarm calls of other species of bird. If the Drongo sees the other birds feeding it will often imitate their alarm calls, frightening them off long enough to fly in and eat the food for itself.

The Common Poorwill, a Nightjar of North America is widely believed to be the only bird in the world that 'hibernates'. In the winter it can enter torpor (strictly speaking not actually hibernation) for most of the season. The native Americans knew all about this, their name for it was the Sleeping One.

The Ancient Murrelet is so adapted to living on water that it has virtually given up on land. The only time it will use land is to lay and incubate its eggs. Within 24 hours or so of hatching the adult bird will lead the chicks off back to the sea. The Ancient Murrelet has come as close as any bird can do to severing its link with land.

THE
END

Birdlife International thinks that 1 in 9 of all bird species are likely to go extinct in the next few decades, that's about 1100 species...
This is a list of the ones that have gone already since 1500. There maybe one or two species on the list that have become extinct via natural means (Island endemics wiped out by Hurricanes, Volcanic eruptions etc) but the vast, vast majority of them have become extinct due to one thing and one thing only – Us, the Human Being. It should also be borne in mind that these are the species that we know about, how many more became extinct before they were known to science?
An asterisk means that the bird is believed to be extinct but is waiting for its fate to be confirmed. The list isn't numbered, the names on the list were so much more than just numbers, they were wonderful living things that we have carelessly wiped out.

English Name	Latin Name
Elephant Bird	Aepyornis maximus/medius
Upland Moa	Megalapteryx didinus
King Island Emu	Dromaius ater
Kangaroo Island Emu	Dromaius baudinianus
Korean Crested Shelduck*	Tadorna cristata
Reunion Shelduck	Alopochen kervazoi
Mauritian Shelduck	Alopochen mauritianus
Amsterdam Duck	Anas marecula
Mauritian Duck	Anas theodori
Mariana Mallard	Anas oustaleti

English Name	Latin Name
Finsch's Duck	*Chenonetta finschi*
Pink-headed Duck*	*Rhodonessa caryophyllacea*
Labrador Duck	*Camptorhynchus labradorius*
Auckland Merganser	*Mergus australis*
Pile-builder Megapode	*Megapodius molistructor*
Viti Levu Scrubfowl	*Megapodius amissus*
New Zealand Quail	*Cortunix novaezelandiae*
Himalayan Quail*	*Ophrysia superciliosa*
Javanese Lapwing*	*Vanellus macropterus*
Tahitian Sandpiper	*Prosobonia leucoptera*
White-winged Sandpiper	*Prosobonia ellisi*
North Island Snipe	*Coenocorypha barrierensis*
South Island Snipe	*Coenocorypha iredalei*
Eskimo Curlew*	*Numenius borealis*
Slender-billed Curlew*	*Numenius tenuirostris*
Great Auk	*Pinguinus impennis*
Canarian Oystercatcher	*Haematopus meadewaldoi*
Antillean Cave-rail	*Nesotrochis debooyi*
Hawkin's Rail	*Diaphorapteryx hawkinsi*
Red Rail	*Aphanapteryx bonasia*
Rodrigues Rail	*Aphanapteryx leguati*

English Name	Latin Name
Bar-winged Rail	*Nesoclopeus paecilopterus*
New Caledonian Rail*	*Gallirallus lafresnayanus*
Wake Island Rail	*Gallirallus wakensis*
Dieffenbach's Rail	*Gallirallus dieffenbachii*
Tongatapu Rail	*Gallirallus hypoleucus*
Chatham Rail	*Cabalus modestus*
Reunion Rail	*Dryolimnas augusti*
Ascension Crake	*Mundia elpenor*
Saint Helena Crake	*Porzana astrictocarpus*
Laysan Rail	*Porzana palmeri*
Hawaiian Rail	*Porzana sandwichensis*
Kosrae Crake	*Porzana monasa*
Saint Helena Swamphen	*Aphanocrex podarces*
Lord Howe Swamphen	*Porphyrio albus*
Reunion Swamphen	*Porphyrio coerulescens*
Marquesas Swamphen	*Porphyrio paepae*
North Island Takahe	*Porphyrio mantelli*
New Caledonia Swamphen	*Porphyrio kukwiedei*
Samoan Wood Rail*	*Gallinula pacifica*
Makira Wood Rail*	*Gallinula silvestris*
Tristan Moorhen	*Gallinula nesiotis*

English Name	Latin Name
Mascarene Coot	Fulica newtoni
Columbian Grebe	Podiceps andinus
Alaotra Grebe	Tachybaptus rufolavatus
Atitlan Grebe	Podilymbus gigas
Bermuda Night Heron	Nyctanassa carcinocatactes
Reunion Night Heron	Nycticorax duboisi
Mauritius Night Heron	Nycticorax mauritianus
Rodrigues Night Heron	Nycticorax megacephalus
Ascension Night Heron	Nycticorax olsoni
New Zealand Little Bittern	Ixobrychus novaezelandiae
Reunion Sacred Ibis	Threskiornis solitarius
Spectacled Cormorant	Phalacrocorax perspicillatus
Small Saint Helena Petrel	Bulweria bifax
Bermuda Shearwater	Puffinus parvus
Large Saint Helena Petrel	Psuedobulweria rupinarium
Jamaica Petrel*	Pterodroma caribbaea
Guadalupe Storm Petrel*	Oceanodroma macrodacyla
Chatham Islands Penguin	Eudyptes sp
Saint Helena Dove	Dysmoropelia dekarchiskos
Passenger Pigeon	Ectopistes migratorius
Bonin Woodpigeon	Columba versicolor

English Name	Latin Name
Ryukyu Woodpigeon	*Columba jouyi*
Reunion Pink Pigeon	*Nesoenas duboisi*
Rodrigues Turtle Dove	*Nesoenas rodericana*
Liverpool Pigeon	*Caloenas maculata*
Sulu Bleeding-heart*	*Gallicolumba menagei*
Norfolk Island Ground-dove	*Gallicolumba norfolciensis*
Tanna Ground-dove	*Gallicolumba ferruginea*
Thick-billed Ground-dove	*Gallicolumba salamonis*
Choiseul Crested Pigeon	*Microgoura meeki*
Red-moustached Fruit-dove	*Ptilinopus mercierii*
Negros Fruit-dove*	*Ptilinopus arcanus*
Mauritius Blue Pigeon	*Alectroencis nitidissima*
Dodo	*Raphus cucullatus*
Rodrigues Solitaire	*Pezophaps solitaria*
New Caledonian Lorikeet*	*Charmosyna diadema*
Norfolk Kaka	*Nestor productus*
Society Parakeet	*Cyanoramphus ulietanus*
Black-fronted Parakeet	*Cyanoramphus zealandicus*
Paradise Parrot	*Psephotus pulcherrimus*
Oceanic Eclectus Parrot	*Eclectus infectus*
Seychelles Parakeet	*Psittacula wardi*

English Name	Latin Name
Newton's Parakeet	*Psittacula exsul*
Thirioux's Grey Parrot	*Psittacula bensoni*
Mascarene Parrot	*Mascarinus mascarinus*
Broad-billed Parrot	*Lophopsittacus mauritianus*
Rodrigues Parrot	*Necropsittacus rodericanus*
Glaucous Macaw*	*Anodorhynchus glaucus*
Cuban Red Macaw	*Ara tricolor*
Carolina Parakeet	*Conuropsis carolinensis*
Guadeloupe Parakeet	*Aratinga labati*
Martinique Amazon	*Amazona martinica*
Guadeloupe Amazon	*Amazona violacea*
Delalandes Coua	*Coua delandei*
Saint Helena Cuckoo	*Nannococcyx psix*
Guadalupe Caracara	*Polyborus lutosus*
Reunion Kestrel	*Falco duboisi*
Reunion Owl	*Mascarenotus grucheti*
Mauritius Owl	*Mascarenotus sauzieri*
Rodrigues Owl	*Mascarenotus murivorus*
Laughing Owl	*Sceloglaux albifacies*
Puerto Rican Barn Owl	*Tyto cavatica*
Bahamam Barn Owl	*Tyto pollens*

English Name	Latin Name
Siau Scops Owl*	*Otus siaoensis*
Jamaican Poorwill*	*Siphornorhis americana*
Coppery Thorntail*	*Discosura letitiae*
Brace's Emerald	*Chlorostilbon bracei*
Gould's Emerald	*Chlorostilban elegans*
Bogota Sunangel	*Heliangelus zusii*
Turquoise-throated Puffleg*	*Eriocnemis godini*
Giant Hoopoe	*Upupa antaois*
Imperial Woodpecker*	*Campephilus imperialis*
Ivory-billed Woodpecker*	*Campephilus principalis*
Stephens Island Wren	*Xenicus lyalli*
Bush Wren	*Xenicus longipes*
Tachira Antpitta*	*Grallaria chthonia*
Kioea	*Chaetoptila angustipluma*
Hawai'i Ōō	*Moho nobilis*
O'ahu Ōō	*Moho apicalis*
Moloka'i Ōō	*Moho bishopi*
Kaua'i Ōō	*Moho braccatus*
Chatham Island Bellbird	*Anthornis melanocephala*
Lord Howe Gerygone	*Gerygone insularis*
Mangarevan Whistler	*Pachycephala gambierana*

English Name	Latin Name
Maupiti Monarch	*Pomarea pomarea*
Eiao Monarch	*Pomarea fluxa*
Nuku Hiva Monarch	*Pomarea nukuhivae*
Ua Poa Monarch	*Pomarea mira*
Guam Flycatcher	*Myiagra freycineti*
Short-toed Nuthatch Vanga	*Hypositta perdita*
North Island Piopio	*Turnagra tanagra*
South Island Piopio	*Turnagra capensis*
Huia	*Heteralocha acutirostris*
White-eyed River Martin*	*Pseudochelidon sirintarae*
Red Sea Swallow*	*Petrochelidon perdita*
Moorea Reed Warbler*	*Acrocephalus longirostris*
Chatham Islands Fernbird	*Bowdleria rufescens*
Lord Howe White-eye	*Zosterops strenuus*
White-chested White-eye	*Zosterops albogularis*
Black-browed Babbler	*Malacocincla perspicillata*
Aldabra Brush-warbler	*Nesillas aldabrana*
Kosrae Island Starling	*Aplonis corvina*
Mysterious Starling	*Aplonis mavornata*
Tasman Starling	*Aplonis fusca*
Pohnpei Starling*	*Aplonis pelzelni*

English Name	Latin Name
Bay Starling	*Aplonis ulietensis*
Bourbon Crested Starling	*Fregilupus varius*
Rodrigues Starling	*Necropsar rodericanus*
Grand Cayman Thrush	*Turdus ravidus*
Bonin Thrush	*Zoothera terrestis*
Amani	*Myadestes woahensis*
Kama'o	*Myadestes myadestinus*
Oloma'o*	*Myadestes lanaiensis*
Cozumel Thrasher*	*Toxostoma guttatum*
Black-lored Waxbill*	*Estrilda nigriloris*
Slender-billed Grackle	*Quiscalus palustris*
Bachman's Warbler*	*Vermivora bachmanii*
Semper's Warbler*	*Leucopeza semperi*
Reunion Fody	*Foudia delloni*
Tawny-headed Mountain Finch*	*Leucosticte sillemi*
Bonin Grosbeak	*Chaunoproctus ferreorostris*
Ōū*	*Psittirostra psittacea*
Lana'i Hookbill	*Dysmorodrepanis munroi*
Pila's Palila	*Loxioides kikuichi*
Lesser Koa Finch	*Rhodacanthus flaviceps*
Greater Koa Finch	*Rhodacanthus palmeri*

English Name	Latin Name
Kona Grosbeak	*Psittirostra kona*
Greater Amakihi	*Hemignathus sagittirostris*
Nukupu'u*	*Hemignathus lucidus*
Hawai'i Akialoa	*Hemignathus obscurus*
Greater Akialoa	*Hemignathus sagittirostris*
Kakawahie	*Paroreomyza flammea*
O'ahu Alauahio*	*Paroreomyza maculata*
Ula-ai-hawane	*Ciridops anna*
Black Mamo	*Drepanis funerea*
Hawai'i Mamo	*Drepanis pacifica*
Po'o-uli	*Melamprosops phaeosoma*
Antioquia Brush-finch*	*Atlapetes blancae*
Bermuda Towhee	*Pipilo naufragus*

If you think that list was too long to have in a book just think how long it will be in a few years if Birdlife International are correct...

About the Author

Ever since a young boy Ian Parsons has been into wildlife. He is fascinated by all aspects of natural history especially birds and trees. Ian spent twenty years working as a Ranger and was lucky enough to work with some of Britain's rarest and most iconic wildlife.

Ian has contributed to, and appeared on, several natural history radio and television programs and also writes articles for wildlife magazines. He has written another book entitled 'A Journey Through A Birder's Thoughts' which is a collection of articles, diary notes, essays and opinions.

In 2012 he started his own bird tour company, Griffon Holidays, which runs tours in the birding paradise of Extremadura in central Spain. To find out more about these tours please visit www.griffonholidays.com

www.ingramcontent.com/pod-product-compliance
Lightning Source LLC
Chambersburg PA
CBHW060203290526
45789CB00003B/1143